THE INTERIOR DESIGN HANDBOOK

OTHER BOOKS BY JOANNA WISSINGER

Lost and Found:
Decorating with Unexpected Objects

Victorian Details

The Best Kit Homes

JOANNA WISSINGER

THE INTERIOR DESIGN HANDBOOK

✦ ✦

ILLUSTRATIONS BY
MICHAEL JONAH ALTSCHULER
ARCHITECT

A ROUNDTABLE PRESS BOOK
AN OWL BOOK ✦ HENRY HOLT AND COMPANY ✦ NEW YORK

Henry Holt and Company, Inc.
Publishers since 1866
115 West 18th Street
New York, New York 10011

Henry Holt® is a registered trademark of
Henry Holt and Company, Inc.

Published in Canada by Fitzhenry & Whiteside Ltd.,
195 Allstate Parkway, Markham, Ontario L3R 4T8.

Library of Congress Cataloging-in-Publication Data
Wissinger, Joanna.
The interior design handbook / Joanna Wissinger;
illustrations by Michael Jonah Altschuler—1st ed.
p. cm.
"An Owl book."
Includes bibliographical references.
1. Interior decoration—Handbooks, manuals, etc. I. Title.
NK2110.W56 1994 94-16289
747—dc20 CIP

ISBN 0-8050-2715-7 (An Owl Book: pbk.)

Henry Holt books are available for special promotions and
premiums. For details contact: Director, Special Markets.

First Edition—1995

DESIGNED BY LUCY ALBANESE

Printed in the United States of America
All first editions are printed on acid-free paper. ∞

10 9 8 7 6 5 4 3 2 1

A Roundtable Press Book
Directors: Marsha Melnick and Susan E. Meyer
Executive Editor: Amy T. Jonak
Project Editor: Virginia Croft

CONTENTS

✦ ✦

HOW TO USE THIS HANDBOOK

✦ ✦

This book is designed in the form of a workbook to help you, the reader, decorate or redecorate your home. It demystifies the often-confusing process of interior design and helps you figure out how to meet your needs and wants while making your home a beautiful, comfortable, and practical place to live.

The Interior Design Handbook is divided into three parts, each with a specific function. The first part, "The Big Picture," covers the fundamentals of planning the decoration or redecoration of anything from a single room to an entire house or apartment, choosing a color scheme, and choosing a style. The information and ideas gained from reading the three chapters in this section—"Developing an Overall Plan," "Creating a New Color Scheme," and "Choosing a Style"—will stand you in good stead whether your home-decorating project is large or small. Here are the basics, including how to take a personal inventory, interview yourself and your family to determine your exact likes and dislikes, plan a budget, schedule a project, and make a room plan; develop the perfect new color scheme for each room or revamp an old one; and select the decorating style, whether casual or formal, best suited to your personality and way of life. Each chapter contains checklists and exercises to help you to determine and accomplish your planning and decorating goals.

Part Two, "Your Home, Room by Room," allows you to take stock of every room in your home, from the living room to the laundry room. Building on the basic concepts and goals established in Part One, each chapter focuses on the decorating problems of an individual room. They contain checklists of key points, topic-by-topic discussions of design elements—including lighting, seating, and storage—and exercises specifically intended to help you work out a room scheme adapted to your personalized needs. Throughout, line drawings clarify the text and illuminate specific points.

The third and final part of *The Interior Design Handbook,* "Specifics," deals in detail with several design topics. Its chapters describe how and where to buy furniture of all types, styles, and materials, from traditional to contemporary; identify and evaluate various window treatments, from simple blinds to lavish draperies, including handling problem windows; explain the particulars of domestic light fixtures; explore the many options for wall and floor coverings, from paint and paper to carpet and parquet; and illustrate how to select and arrange decorative objects to the best effect, including how to frame and hang pictures and photos. Appendixes give information on hiring and working with a professional designer or decorator, as well as sample budgets and costs.

Don't be shy about really using this handbook. If you do, you'll find it to be an invaluable reference and record of your new home design. The exercises and checklists interspersed throughout the text were developed with exactly this purpose in mind. So make them work for you—fill out the charts and answer the questionnaires, complete the exercises and ponder the checklists carefully. Make notes in the margins and tuck in inspirational photos, paint chips, and wallpaper samples. Make it work for you, and it will help you create the living spaces that are perfect for you and your family.

PART ONE

THE BIG PICTURE

1

DEVELOPING AN OVERALL PLAN

Successful home decorating involves practicality and comfort as well as good looks and style. Of course you want your home to reflect your individual taste, but also you must discover exactly what you need, what you would like to improve, how you would decorate if money were not a consideration, and how much you can actually afford to do. Starting with the ideal, you can then work back to a realistic budget, sort out your priorities, and decide which steps to take. The problem is not to do too much or too little but to do the right things, the things that really make a difference.

TAKING A PERSONAL INVENTORY

Begin by interviewing yourself, your spouse or partner, and your kids about practical, aesthetic, and budgetary matters in order to get a firm grasp of what you have to work with. Ask yourself certain obvious questions: What sort of life do you lead? Do you entertain much? Do you prefer large parties or intimate gatherings, or do you have family over just for holiday dinners? What do you do in each room? Then answer the questions in the following exercises and discuss them with your family.

EXERCISES

1. How long do you plan to stay in your present home? This answer will help you decide the best areas in which to invest your decorating budget. See page 26 for more on this topic.

2. Do you have children, or are you planning to start a family? How many? What are their ages? Will your children be leaving home soon?

3. Do other family members live with you? Is this a possibility in the future? For example, will you need to add hand rails, grab bars, and special door hardware to accommodate elderly relatives who will come to live with you or stay on long visits?

4. How much space (number of rooms) do you anticipate needing (for example, three family bedrooms, guest room, home office, kitchen, family room/TV room, formal dining room, living room)? Can you use existing space, including a remodeled attic or basement, or will you need to add on?

5. Do you have pets? Which rooms do they go into? Are they allowed on the furniture? You'll need to consider the needs and habits of your pets when choosing upholstery, floor coverings, and finishes for your home.

6. Where does your family like to eat—kitchen, family room, or dining room? How many meals do you cook each week? This will help you in the practical planning of cooking and eating areas.

7. To discover and avert any conflicts and plan for necessary double-duty areas, make a list of possible multiple uses for rooms. For example, kitchen: cooking, eating, paying bills, doing homework or hobbies, watching TV, visiting.

8. How often do you entertain, and in what style? For example, do you have large cocktail parties, intimate dinners, formal dinner parties, informal buffets? Which room do you use most? Are you pleased with it or do you want to change it? How?

9. Is there enough sleeping and private space for everyone in the family? What needs to be added?

10. Make a list of your family's regular leisure activities performed at home, such as reading, watching TV, exercising, sewing, woodworking, and piano playing.

____

____

____

____

____

____

____

____

11. Do you need a laundry room or a hobby room?

12. Do you have enough storage space? List what you need to store (books, out-of-season clothing, sports equipment, and so forth). Make a list of special areas where you might need to store large equipment (freezer, weight machine, loom, or other equipment).

13. Do you and those with whom you share your living space have the same taste or different tastes? If different, have you agreed on how to reconcile the differences? (Does one of you get one room, one the other? How have you compromised?) Can you blend your tastes and possessions? See pages 18–21 for a list of topics you should discuss with your family and pages 22–24 for a child's inventory of likes and dislikes.

14. Have you thought of a color scheme? Do you have a favorite color? Which colors make you happy? Which ones don't you like? For more on this subject see Chapter 2, "Creating a New Color Scheme."

15. Do you want a traditional, formal decor or something more modern and contemporary? Or do you prefer a casual country look?

16. What look would go best with the style of your house? Light and bright? Modern? A period style, such as Georgian or Victorian? See Chapter 3, "Choosing a Style," for more possibilities.

17. Do you own a standout piece—an heirloom or flea market or auction find—around which you could base a scheme? An antique textile, a family portrait, a Victorian sofa? Do you have a favorite fabric that might make a good start for developing a color scheme? List possibilities here.

18. Ignoring price, list ten luxuries that would improve your home and that you desire most.

    1. ______________________________

    2. ______________________________

    3. ______________________________

    4. ______________________________

    5. ______________________________

    6. ______________________________

    7. ______________________________

    8. ______________________________

    9. ______________________________

    10. ______________________________

19. What's the most you can (or want to) spend? (Keep in mind that to be safe you should build an extra 20 percent into your budget; things often end up costing more than you think they will.) In this chapter you will learn how to work out a budget. For now, state the total amount you have set aside to spend.

20. Is this total based on guesswork or have you actually priced what things will cost? If you have to cut your budget, what sort of compromises will be acceptable? Are you willing to find less expensive alternatives for some items? Rather than compromise, would you prefer to postpone some of the improvements you can't afford now?

21. Do you or does anyone in your household have do-it-yourself skills, such as carpentry, painting, or woodworking? List them here.

____

____

____

____

____

____

GETTING IDEAS: SOURCES OF INSPIRATION

Decorating plans should be influenced by the architectural style and proportions of a house or apartment, where it's located (in a city or a small town; by a lake, in the woods, or set on a lawn), and how much natural light it receives.

Your home should be treated with respect, and all of its existing elements should be used to their best advantage, including the doors, windows, staircases, fireplaces, good views, decorative materials, the proportions of existing rooms, the moldings, and any other architectural details.

To absorb the character of a new house or apartment, you have to take your time. Top interior designers often tell their clients to live in a house or apartment for a while without doing anything. Put up blinds or shades for privacy but don't worry about new curtains. Get to know the space and its proportions, which features you want to emphasize, and which you want to disguise. Once you develop a feeling for the interior, you can begin to visualize the colors you want to use, what new pieces of furniture to buy, and how furniture might be arranged.

Of course, if you're redecorating a home you've lived in for a while, you probably have lots of ideas for changes. You may want to strip and refinish the painted woodwork in the dining room, buy a new sofa and install track lighting in the living room, replace the atomic-style 1950s overhead light fixture in the kitchen with something more modern and to your own taste, or take out the old linoleum and put in something brighter and fresher. The problem then is to sort out your ideas and decide which ones to implement.

Look through decorating magazines and style books to get an idea of the result you're aiming for. While it's unlikely that you'll see an interior exactly like the one you want to create, you will be exposed to a number of appealing possibilities. Visit local decorating shops and furniture showrooms for prospective materials—carpeting, wallcoverings, flooring, and fabrics—and collect samples and brochures. Catalogs also can be a good source, from Spiegel to Crate & Barrel. Cut out pictures from magazines and catalogs and gather together your samples of wallpaper, upholstery fabric, paint—whatever strikes your fancy. Don't worry whether or not things go together. That can wait for later.

Create a master file for all of your pictures, your collection of samples, and notes or lists of sources that you've made. Every time you make a change in the source of a piece, in your color scheme, or in your window treatment, for example, indicate the date and put the changed document in the file. It's a good idea to keep a record of everything so that you don't lose track of details or forget a good idea. You'll find that decisions are easier if you at least try to be organized. It will also enable you to see the path you have taken and old ideas that you might want to return to later. At some point, spread out your pictures and samples on a flat surface or pin them up on a large bulletin board so that you can view them all at once. That way you'll see what goes together and what you can eliminate right away, and you'll form some definite ideas about what you want to keep.

If you get in the habit of carrying around a small notebook, you can jot down notes or make little sketches of any ideas you have about furniture arrangement or window treatments or such. You don't have to be an artist—the sketches are simply to help jog your memory later. Otherwise you might have a brilliant inspiration on your way to work on the commuter train or waiting at a red light and not be able to remember it later. This might seem like a lot of work, but it will prove worthwhile in the long run. Even if you are working with a design professional who will be doing all of the legwork, you need to give him or her an idea of what to look for—and you're the only one who can tell the designer what you want.

Try to be flexible. Things that you have set your heart on may prove impossible to obtain or may not work out the way you thought they would. Remember that while good interior design will contribute to the comfort and ease of your life, it should not be an end in itself. Take comfort from these two decorating truths: too-perfect rooms are as boring as too-perfect people, and the most successful decorating is the result of careful editing.

MAKING A FLOOR PLAN

By accurately measuring the dimensions of your living space, you will get a clear idea of exactly what you have to work with. In order to decorate, you must know what you are decorating—how many rooms, how many square feet, how many windows, and so on. If you don't have a floor plan of your house or apartment, it will be worth your time to make one. In fact, drawing a plan of your living space is the foundation for a comprehensive interior design.

Most plans are drawn to scale (which means you will have to measure everything very accurately) and show rooms from above. They generally show things like window and door openings and electrical outlets, but they don't show anything on the ceiling, such as ceiling fixtures (although these can be

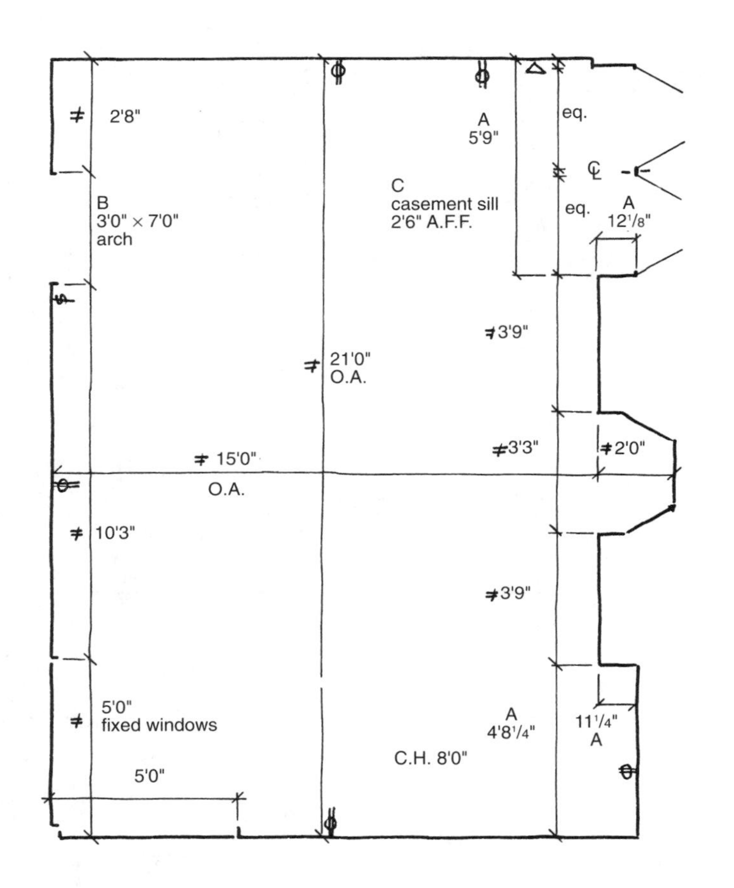

indicated if you like). Architects use symbols for various details, and you may want to use some of them too (see illustration on page 16).

Measure the room using a tape measure or a carpenter's rule. If your tape measure isn't long enough, you can use a roll of string or twine. If you're going to do a lot of measuring, you might want to buy a heavy-duty tape measure, the kind that contractors and architects use. It will spare you a lot of aggravation.

It's important that measuring be done accurately because many decisions—furniture size and arrangement, wall-covering and fabric yardage, the amount of carpet you buy—are going to depend on it. Measuring works best with two people. The old craftsman's adage "Measure twice, cut once" is worth remembering. You can save yourself a lot of time and grief that way.

Field Measurements

A. *Measurements at these points should be exact in anticipation of built-ins or furniture that will fit into the recess.*

B. *Careful measurement of the opening into the room as well as the path leading to it is critical in determining that furniture, such as a piano, will pass through openings. Other measurements are shown as ≠ (approximate).*

C. *If you plan to put something below the sill, be sure to measure the height of the sill.*

D. *Calculations of room areas are necessary when estimating costs for floor coverings or ordering paint. Use these equations:*

ROOM (FLOOR) AREA:

Multiply the overall (O.A.) length by the overall width of the room.

21'0" × 15'0" = 315 square feet

WALL AREA:

Multiply the sum of all the lengths of the walls by the ceiling height (C.H.).

15'0" + 21'0" × 2 = 72'0" × 8'0" = 576 square feet

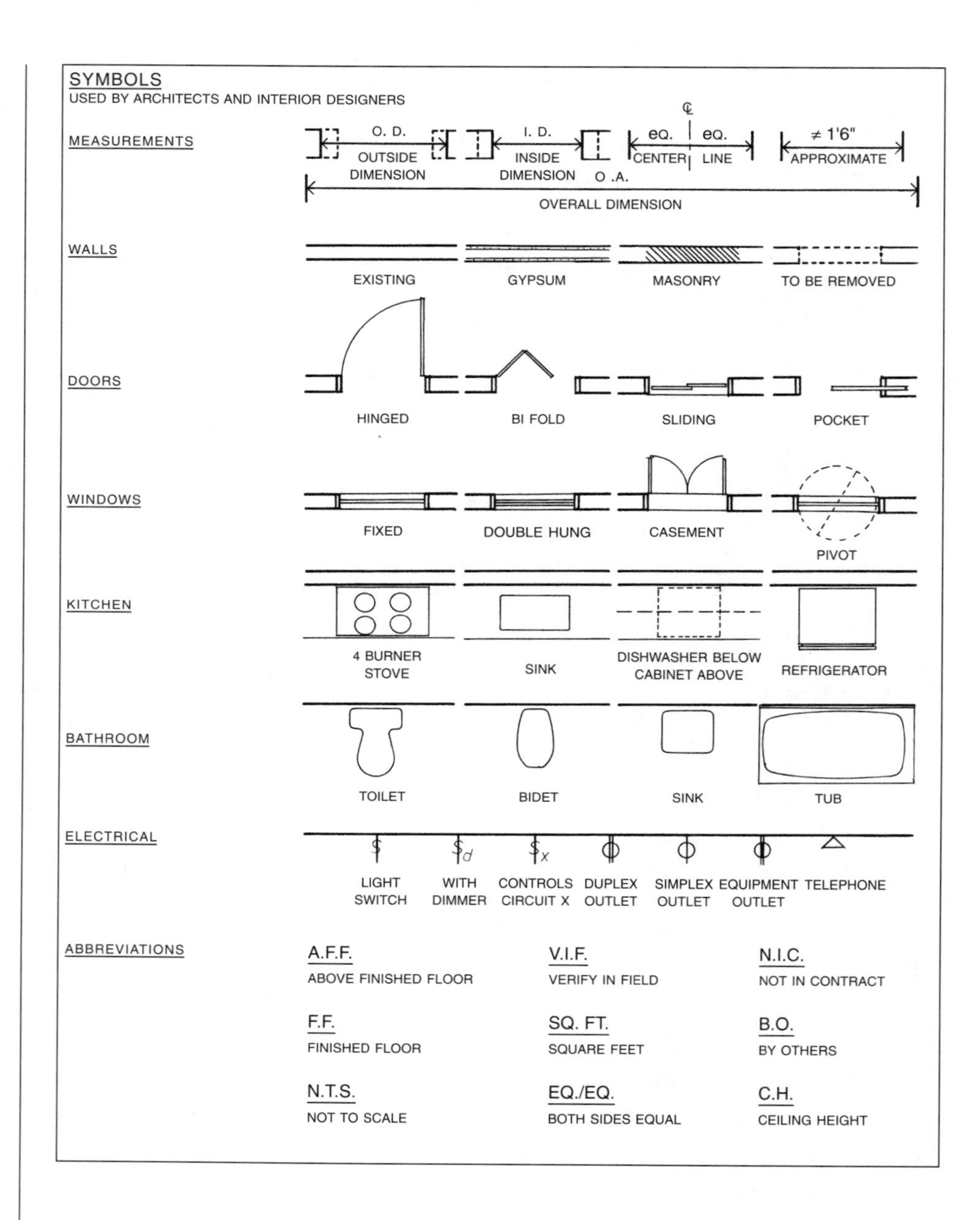

It's probably easiest to start with one room. First draw a rough sketch and mark all of the dimensions—length, width, and height—on it as you measure. Then draw a floor plan to scale on a sheet of graph paper. Decide on a scale; if you have a lot of details, you may want to use a one-inch to one-foot scale on a large sheet of paper in order to get everything in. Use a sharp pencil with fairly hard lead to draw your plan; this prevents smudging. Be sure to include more than just the dimensions of the room: also indicate the positions of windows, doors, electrical outlets, telephone jacks, radiators, pipes, and other permanent features, such as fireplaces, closets, air conditioners, and any built-in furniture.

Once you know the dimensions of your room, you can determine how much paint or wallpaper or flooring you will need to buy. To find the area of the floor (which is usually also the area of the ceiling, if it is parallel to the floor), multiply the length of the room by the width. To find the area of a wall, multiply the height by the length. A quick way to find the wall area for an entire room is to measure the perimeter and multiply it by the ceiling height. Subtract for windows and doors if there are a lot of them; otherwise don't bother.

The correct measurement of doors and windows is critical when it comes to moving large pieces of furniture in and out of a room. If you live in an apartment building, you should also measure the elevator. That way your new king-size bed or armoire won't have to go back where it came from because it can't fit through the door!

Next you can add your furniture, either drawing in each piece by hand or using cut-out silhouettes. You can make these yourself, cutting out pieces of a slightly heavier paper stock, or use a kit that supplies you with a variety of furniture silhouettes done to scale. (These come with their own graph paper and can be found at hardware and home do-it-yourself stores, such as Home Depot.) You can easily move the cutouts around, saving the backs and patience of everyone involved in the decorating scheme.

Make plenty of photocopies of the completed plan, as you will need them for various purposes. Take a copy of your plan and list of dimensions with you when you shop. Before you buy a piece of furniture or a rug, measure it and jot down its dimensions. Go home and make a cutout to scale of the piece and try it out on your plan. This may seem like a lot of bother, but it's better than bearing the cost of making a big mistake. If you need to make a quick decision (at a warehouse sale or an auction, for example), at least have a preliminary idea of the size and scale of the piece you think might fill your empty space. That way you'll be less likely to make mistakes. Improvisation can be an important part of decorating, but without a good plan you'll soon lose control.

It's also a good idea to take color photographs of your home with you while you shop. An on-staff decorator may spot an opportunity that you have overlooked.

INVOLVING FAMILY MEMBERS

If you live with other people, they should be consulted about decorating plans, for they have needs and preferences that must be considered. In the exercises at the beginning of this chapter, there is a question (number 13) about handling different tastes among people who live together. You might want to consult with your partner or spouse about color schemes as well. Use the space here to interview other household members for their thoughts about decorating.

EXERCISES

1. Favorite colors:

2. Favorite materials:

3. Favorite styles:

4. Decorating dislikes (in general):

5. What do they like best about the existing design or past decorating schemes?

6. How do they feel the current decor could be improved?

7. Ask them to look through decorating magazines or your collection of clippings and samples and make separate piles of things they like and dislike. It is important to define what they like about each picture in order to integrate it into your overall design.

8. What atmosphere do they want to create in each room? What activities do they imagine taking place in individual rooms? Ask them to make a room-by-room list.

DECORATING FOR CHILDREN

It's important to involve children in decorating as well, although younger children will probably not have the attention span to go through the process described above. Most children, no matter how young, will definitely want to participate in decorating their own bedrooms and play spaces.

It's important to put aside, as much as possible, any fantasies *you* might have about a room for your youngster. Listen to what your child wants. For example, he or she might pick a color scheme of purple and orange, which you find repulsive, but don't put your foot down and demand red and blue. Instead find a way to incorporate the colors your child chooses into an overall scheme. Most kids are perfectly willing to state their likes and dislikes and then live with their choices.

It's especially important to remember these rules when confronted with recalcitrant teenagers. Some of their ideas may seem ridiculous to you, but teenagers deserve just as much respect as any three-year-old when it comes to having what they want in their rooms. Don't do what so many parents do—let the teenager exist in a disorderly mess of clothing, books, and CDs amid the remnants of a childhood decor, closed to view by a perpetually shut door.

As near adults, teens need to have their autonomy and their privacy (and are very touchy about protecting them). Involve your teenage son or daughter in creating a personal space, and try not to be too rigid about what he or she can or cannot do. Allow for improvisation—create a corkboard wall for posters or a wall that can be written and painted on. Wall-to-wall carpeting, acoustical ceiling tile, and a set of headphones will let them make as much noise as they want. Make sure that the room is practical, with plenty of storage space, a study area, and a comfortable bed. Other than that, let them do their own thing—paying attention, of course, to the budget.

So consult your youngster (of any age from two to eighteen) about color schemes and room themes. If you have a specific idea in mind, show your child a photograph or draw a picture and get his or her reactions. If there is a choice between two fabrics or colors, let the child make the final decision. While the end result might not be the storybook room that you envisioned, rest assured that by allowing your child to participate in decorating his or her own room, you are promoting a sense of accomplishment and empowerment that will last into adulthood.

EXERCISES

Child's Personal Inventory

Sit down with your child and conduct a personal inventory, just as you did for yourself.

1. Favorite colors:

2. Favorite cartoon characters or superheroes:

3. Favorite activities:

4. Other favorite themes:

5. How much storage is needed for your child's possessions (books, toys, clothing, sports equipment, and such)?

6. What about school and study needs? How much space is needed for a desk, computer, and so on?

7. Does your child need space to play with friends or to have friends stay overnight?

You must be practical as well as creative when decorating for young children. One of the first considerations is safety. All materials that go into decorating a child's room or a room that is frequently used by a child must be nontoxic and fireproof. Check labels carefully and follow all instructions when using paints and adhesives. Make sure that you keep all toxic materials, such as solvents, locked up and out of the way. Similarly, keep tools out of the reach of children.

The second important consideration for a household with children is ease of care. You will probably not want to have silk upholstery and white carpeting. What you need are materials that are durable and easy to clean. You can get a head start by checking your present indoor environment for signs of wear, such as ripped upholstery, a stained or soiled carpet, or scuff marks on the walls. Make a list of the problems you find, then make a corresponding list of remedies. For example, you might decide to reupholster the couch in more durable fabric, replace the carpet with a stain-resistant type, make the baseboards higher, and repaint, or repaper with a washable wall covering. A list will help you prioritize your decorating choices.

ACCOMMODATING PETS

What do your pets need? Probably a place to eat, a place to sleep, and some way to get in and out, such as a pet door (those who live in apartments will have to make other arrangements). Again, easy-care materials are key. Avoid light-colored carpets in areas with heavy pet traffic. Certain fiber and texture types, such as sisal, Berber, or carved pile, are much harder to remove stains from. Even stain-guarded carpet isn't guaranteed against vomit. Wood floors are fairly easy to clean and can be finished in polyurethane to prevent staining or fading as the result of pet accidents. Vinyl and tile floors are the most durable but aren't always practical for use throughout the house.

A sheet or blanket draped over a sofa or chair provides protection so that a dog or cat can curl up on it, and it can be removed when guests come over. Most cats are attracted to terry cloth and will choose to lie wherever a towel is placed. Another, somewhat more graceful, solution is to use slipcovers in a washable or dry-cleanable fabric that has been treated with a stain guard. Cats in particular like to get their claws into heavy-weave fabrics, such as tapestry prints; it's a good idea to cover these with a "pet drape" (but an even better idea is to train your cat to use a scratching post from the beginning—or to have the cat declawed). Try to keep pet hair under control with frequent brushing and vacuuming.

Leather upholstery is another option, although it's expensive; it wears well, ages wonderfully, and seems impervious to fur (but not to teeth and claws). Tightly woven fabrics like velvet also do well, although you must be diligent about removing any fur accumulation promptly. The best method, although difficult, may be to keep your pets off the furniture altogether or allow them on only a single piece, which can be draped with a sheet. Dogs who like to gnaw furniture legs should be distracted with a new chew toy when the new table or chair comes home.

Covered litter boxes (either the kind that looks like a small Quonset hut or the more elaborate dollhouse type) will give cats privacy in style. They are also a boon to apartment dwellers, who often have no place to put this necessary cat accessory except in the bathroom, where it sits in full view, detracting from the decor of that room. Another solution is to conceal the box behind a piece of furniture or simple screen (make sure the cat knows how to find it).

LOOKING AHEAD

How will your future plans affect your decorating ideas? If you don't plan to stay in your current home very long, you probably won't want to pour a lot of money into window treatments and new flooring. Conversely, if this is where you plan to live for the rest of your life, it is probably a wise investment to spend money on built-in storage, for example, or new carpeting.

Don't think just about money, though. If you plan to spend several years in the same home, it pays to make your decorating scheme flexible enough to accommodate future changes. For example, the guest bedroom might well become a nursery. Start out on the right path with plenty of storage space and durable materials. If you're close to retirement age and plan to spend your free time traveling rather than doing housework, you'll want a home that's easy to maintain and doesn't require a lot of fuss. If you'll be spending a great deal more time at home, perhaps you'll need a study more than a formal dining room. All of these things should be considered when drawing up a decorating plan.

DEVELOPING A BUDGET

The first thing you need to find out is how much everything will cost. Once you've figured out a basic plan and have an idea of what you need, spend some time on the phone or at the local home improvement or decorating store to get a rough estimate of costs. If you can come up with a rough but fairly detailed idea of what you want—say, a new sofa, new slipcovers for armchairs, repainted woodwork, new wallpaper, and two new window treatments—along with the appropriate dimensions, a designer or decorating service will be able to give you a price quote fairly quickly, especially if you need only a ballpark figure.

Next, get the framework of your home into good working order before you decorate. If you own your home, this is a sound investment. If you are a renter, you may prefer to stick to changes you can take with you when you move. It is a waste of time to do a glamorous makeover if the roof is about to fall in. At this point you may have to backtrack and wait until you've made necessary repairs and renovations before you start redecorating.

You've drawn a plan of the room or rooms you are redecorating, so you know what you've got to work with and have an idea of what needs to be done. Refer back to your personal inventory (pages 4–12) to remind yourself of your initial budget figure (which may have changed). Sit down with your financial records and figure out how much money you can spend and how best to use it. Make a list of what you feel are the essentials, in order of importance. Follow the example in the first paragraph of this section: replace the sofa, have slipcovers made for two armchairs, repaint the woodwork, put up new wallpaper, and get new window treatments for two windows. Then write down how much each will cost, and you'll soon discover what's really essential.

Aside from the cost of the items themselves, you'll need to add in the cost of subcontractors—electricians, carpenters, paperhangers, painters. Check with your insurance company on whether you need to increase your coverage if you will have outsiders working in your home. Remember to add in a contingency fund for emergencies, about 20 percent of the whole. A good budget will help you get your priorities straight so that you can begin to think about alternatives and will tell you where you need to do more research. Use the "Making a Budget" exercise at the end of this chapter as a worksheet.

Inevitably, unless you're very fortunate, you will have to cut back on your budget. Review your personal inventory to remind yourself of your priorities. Sit and think about what you want and need, and instead of getting a new sofa right away, put a sheet over your hideous old sofa and stop worrying about it. That way you won't make a mistake out of impatience and then a few months later wonder what you're going to do with a bunch of ill-planned purchases, while your plaster is flaking, your sink is discoloring, and your window is admitting a draft.

To cut back your budget, first figure out what is truly essential. Maybe it's comfortable seating. This is a place to spend money, and a sofa is a major purchase that will last a long time. Curtains, on the other hand, are not essential; if you need privacy or to block out light, inexpensive miniblinds can suffice until you can afford to invest in something more to your liking. Lighting is another essential—you need to be able to see! Lighting also has a psychological effect on many people. Proper lighting assures that everyone who uses a room will feel at ease. Better to have too few things at first than a lot of stuff that you don't like. Sorting out your options is one of your first steps, and one of the most important should be enjoying the rooms you live in.

You probably don't have the luxury of starting completely from scratch and being able to have everything you want. Very few people do. Most people already own things they like and want (or need) to keep, so their decorating plan needs to include these things. Use them as starting points for your new scheme. If you're moving into a new place, however, you may discover that your beloved old possessions, while far too good to throw out, simply don't fit in the new place. In such a case, you have a few choices: you can have a garage sale to sell the old stuff and use the proceeds for new furniture; you can put the old things in storage and buy new ones, your wallet protesting all the while; or you can figure out a way to revamp your old things to fit their new situation. For example, you can buy or have a slipcover made for your old sofa and add lots of pillows. You can restyle your old curtains. New accessories, such as table lamps, vases, and picture frames, will make a difference too. A dramatic palm or tall ficus tree, a new rug, or even a decorative tablecloth on an occasional table are all relatively inexpensive ways to give a room a new look. But you still have to plan.

SCHEDULING BASICS

If you draw up a working schedule before you begin, even if you are doing only one room, you will be able to coordinate everything better.

First, take care of the mechanical details. If you need new electrical outlets or phone jacks or if the plumber has to come in, plan to complete these tasks before you start painting, have new carpeting installed, or hang new curtains. Workers usually make a mess, and you can't always count on them to clean up after themselves. Their priority is getting that pipe in, not sparing the brand-new carpet.

The general sequence for subcontractors in a residential renovation would be as follows. This list will help you plan when to bring in each person.

Subcontractor	*Task*
Electrician, plumber	Disconnects
Demolition crew	Removes and carts
Electrician, plumber	Roughs-in electrical, plumbing, heating, and air-conditioning
Carpenter	Walls and door openings
Tile setter	Floors and walls
Lather	Tape and plaster
Painter, paperhanger	Paint and wallpaper
Floor installer	Refinishes wood, installs flooring (wood, vinyl, cork)
Cabinetmaker	Installs built-ins
Electrician, plumber	Finishes hookups
Painter	Touches up
Carpet installer	Lays carpets
Decorative trades	Prepare finishes
Movers	Move furniture

CHECKLIST: *Suggested Schedule for Decorating a Single Room*

PHASE ONE

1. Make your design scheme final.
2. Draw up plans to scale.
3. Calculate amounts of materials needed (paint, wallpaper, tile, carpet, and so on), and order them.
4. Order or start making new soft furnishings, such as curtains and slipcovers.

PHASE TWO

1. Warn neighbors of activity (especially if you live in an apartment building), and check availability of the elevator.

(continued)

2. Roll up your rugs or cover up wall-to-wall carpets. Remove all fittings, such as switch plates or window hardware. Cover things that can't be removed with plastic or fabric drop cloths and tape. Dust from wallboard and plaster is very invasive.
3. Have new outlets and jacks put in, and new plumbing, if necessary.
4. Prepare the room (move furniture away from walls, cover it with sheets, and so forth).

PHASE THREE

1. Prepare surfaces. Strip wallpaper off walls or sand old floor in preparation for refinishing. Scrape walls for painting, spackle holes, tape moldings, and so on.
2. Put up new decorative moldings.
3. Install new built-in units.
4. Prime surfaces. Apply undercoat.

PHASE FOUR

1. Paint ceilings, then walls, then woodwork.
2. If papering, paint woodwork first.
3. Treat floor (bleach or stain flooring, if necessary).
4. Put down new carpets or flooring.
5. Fix lighting, replace fittings.
6. Hang new or refurbished window treatments.
7. Put furniture in place.

EXERCISES

EVALUATING WHAT NEEDS TO BE DONE

It's a good idea to make a chart of the room's different elements. Always date your charts so that if you make more than one, you can tell which is the latest.

Make a list down the left side that includes lighting, electrical outlets, heating units, walls, ceiling, floor, windows, furniture, and other elements in the room. Then across the top make column headings for noting the present condition, changes that need to be made, how you're going to treat them decoratively, and the cost. You might also want a column for noting the last time the room was painted, when the furniture was bought, how old the carpet is, and so on. Keep a schedule of paint colors (brand, number, finish, oil or latex).

For example, reading across the "floors" entry, your notations might be: "Floor boards in bad condition, color uneven, some splintering," followed by, "Have stripped, sanded, filled, restained, and polished." A decorative treatment might include the purchase of an area rug or the addition of a stenciled border. Peeling paint on the ceiling would mean having it scraped and repainted. If you are repairing a fault, you may not need to add anything to the third column. In the fourth column, keep a note of how much the change will cost.

Workday and Weekend Schedules

Complete the following schedules to determine which rooms you use the most. They will help you get a complete picture of how and where you spend your time and can help you visualize what changes in your decorating scheme might make your life easier, as well as aid in deciding what to tackle first.

Describe a typical workday schedule for your household.

	Activity	*Room Used*
Morning:		
Afternoon:		
Evening:		

Describe a typical weekend schedule.

	Activity	*Room Used*
Morning:		
Afternoon:		
Evening:		

Making a Budget

Use the following sample list for a living room as a model for constructing your budget. Not all of these suggested items will apply to your own project. For example, you may not be hiring a subcontractor or decorator, but you probably will want to create a detailed breakdown of exactly what materials and furniture need to be purchased (see "Developing a Budget," page 26).

Budget Items	*Estimated Cost*	*Amount Budgeted*
Furniture		
sofa	________	________
chair(s)	________	________
ottoman	________	________
coffee table	________	________
end table(s)	________	________
other	________	________
Built-in units		
cabinets	________	________
credenzas	________	________
bookshelves	________	________
other	________	________

Budget Items	*Estimated Cost*	*Amount Budgeted*
Lighting		
ceiling fixture	______	______
table or floor lamp(s)	______	______
outlets, rewiring	______	______
Floors		
carpet or rugs	______	______
tile	______	______
sanding and staining	______	______
Walls and ceiling		
paint	______	______
wallpaper	______	______
molding	______	______
other	______	______
Fabric		
upholstery	______	______
curtains	______	______
other	______	______
Do-it-yourself equipment rental	______	______
Decorator's fee	______	______
Subcontractors' fees (painter, carpenter, electrician, other labor)	______	______
Insurance policy (if necessary)	______	______
Contingency fund (20 percent of total)	______	______
TOTAL	______	______

Use your personal inventory and the exercises as background information to create your overall decorating plan. You'll also find it helpful to refer back to your personal inventory as you read the following chapters.

Spot's Big Book
of Words

2

CREATING A NEW COLOR SCHEME

Color catches the eye. While other, more subtle, elements may be equally important in creating an overall decorative scheme, color is definitely what is noticed first. Color has a strong effect on an interior. It can change the feeling of a room, making it seem larger or smaller, warmer or cooler. Color also affects the emotions. Various colors can make a room appear cool and restful or warm and stimulating.

Color can also cause problems. Many people feel timid about choosing and working with color, so they have difficulty making decisions and getting started on this important decorating step. Some people find that they like several colors equally and simply can't choose among them, while others find it hard just to find one color they like well enough to live with.

Acquiring the confidence to work with color does take some perseverance, but it's worth the effort. People who lack this assuredness often choose bland schemes that they are not completely happy with. Since decorating is expensive, and you can end up living with a mistake for a long time, you may be tempted to stick to the tried and true. This can be a mistake in itself.

The best approach to color is to be analytical. Start thinking about and noticing color. When you see a color combination you like, consider carefully why you like it and how you might re-create it in your home. It might be in a garden or an urban scene; it might be from a vintage dress print or an antique pillow, a scene from a favorite vacation site, a corner of a friend's home, or a painting spotted in an art gallery.

Become conscious of color wherever you go. Make color a separate section in your clippings file (see page 13). Magazines and books that specialize in decorating are great sources of color ideas. Even if they show schemes that are far too expensive or theatrical for your home, they can provide food for thought. Gather everything that appeals to you and study the clippings to see what each scheme has in common. You might discover that you are most attracted to dark colors and homespun textures—a countrified, relaxed look. Or perhaps you'll find yourself leaning toward light, bright colors and shiny surfaces—an urban, sophisticated look. Or maybe you'll fall somewhere in between. Be guided by your choices; you will feel comfortable with them. Color schemes are constrained by practicality and enlivened by serendipity. Above all, trust your own taste.

CHOOSING COLORS

Color choice is basic to your decorating scheme. The imaginative use of color will ensure that your room is a success. You need to learn the simple rules of color to do a good job. An effective color scheme obeys certain basic rules having to do with the physical and psychological aspects of color. Very few people are such good judges of color that they can tell instantly whether or not different shades will go together. Most of us have to work at developing a sense of color.

Fortunately, ready-made color combinations abound, both in nature and in things made by people, such as artworks, textiles, stained glass, and ceramics. You may already own something—a painting, a rug, a pillow or bedspread—that you want to use as the basis for a color scheme. If you collect furniture or decorative objects of a certain era or if you live in an older home, you may want to use a color scheme that's true to the period. Historically accurate color schemes can be found in museum re-creations and in books on historic decoration and period style. Many manufacturers now produce lines of paint, fabric, and wallcoverings in historically correct colors and patterns.

It's fairly easy to find fabrics and patterns in colors that you like if your color scheme employs colors that are in vogue (blue is a perennially popular color, for example). If you want something offbeat or unusual, you may have to search it out. Try alternative sources, such as dress fabrics or flea markets. You may be lucky enough to discover a cache of discontinued fabric at the discount upholstery fabric store, or you may have to depend on what's available from the local furniture or department store and liven it up with unusual accessories.

COLOR AND LIGHT

Color and light have a close relationship. Color, of course, is reflected light, but we are concerned with the effect of light on color. In considering a color scheme, keep in mind what kind of light your room receives. Northern and eastern light have a cool, bluish-white cast that can make a room seem chilly. Warm colors can counteract this tendency. A room that faces west receives warm, golden, late-afternoon sunlight and the rich colors of sunset; cool tones can balance this effect. Conversely, warm tones in a west-facing room can make it seem even cozier.

A room that is seen mostly at night—one used for entertaining, for example—will probably be seen by most people in artificial light. Certain colors look better than others in artificial light because such light is generally less bright than sunlight and tends to have a bluish cast. In it, pinks can look violet, reds appear maroon, and blues can take on a greenish tinge. Although there are color-corrected incandescent bulbs, they are expensive and therefore impractical for most households.

The best way to avoid mistakes and make sure that the color you choose looks good is to get a large swatch or sample of the color and look at it under the light conditions in which it will most often be seen. Buy a yard of upholstery fabric and drape it over the chair or sofa you are re-covering. Take home a carpet sample or tack up a wallpaper swatch. When choosing a paint color, buy the smallest quantity you can and either paint a large section of the wall or, if you prefer, paint a large panel (thirty by forty-eight inches is a good size) of Masonite or heavy-duty cardboard. (Remember to use an undercoat if the board is a dark color.) One more thing: beware of choosing colors in store light. Most stores are lit with fluorescent lights, which tend to make colors appear washed out and seem paler or cooler than they really are.

Color and Proportion

Color affects a room's visual proportions. The rule of thumb is that pale colors make walls and large pieces of furniture appear to recede, so that rooms seem larger, while bright or dark tones seem to bring walls in closer and make large objects appear even bigger. These visual effects have practical applications: a small room appears large if the walls are painted in light tones or white, while a long, narrow room will assume more pleasing proportions if one of the short walls is painted a bright or dark color that contrasts with the other walls. A high ceiling "comes down" when painted a slightly darker tone. Of course, if you love deep colors, go ahead and use them, even in a small room. Better a cozy room you're happy with than a more expansive pastel room that you detest.

These color contrasts don't have to be dramatic or obtrusive in order to work. You don't have to paint a high ceiling black—a deeper tone of the wall color will do. The reverse is true for a low ceiling—painting it white or a lighter tone of the wall color will make it appear higher. Large pieces of furniture will appear to blend in and become much less conspicuous if covered or painted the same color as the walls; conversely, a small piece will stand out more if it is in a bright accent tone.

The eye-fooling properties of color can also be used to spotlight particular features. You can accent architectural details, such as moldings or fireplaces, with a contrasting color to draw attention to them. On the other hand, if they are ugly, in bad shape, or tend to break up the flow of space, paint them the same color as the walls to make them blend in.

Color and Emotion

Colors have an emotional temperature and temperamental effect. Warm colors seem exciting and active; cool colors, restful and soothing. Intensity of color has a similar effect: pastel colors, no matter their temperature, are soothing, while deep colors or hues, whether red or blue, are exciting and stimulating.

Reds, yellows, and oranges are "warm" hues. Blues, greens, and grays are "cool" hues. However, a yellow that moves toward green will be cool. White and black are generally regarded as neutrals, as are beige, taupe, and other variations on brown. Gray added to warm colors makes them cooler. White or yellow added to cool colors warms them up.

Colors have other emotional connotations and connections. For example, yellow, the color of the sun, is seen as perky and lively. Green not only is the color of leaves and grass and other natural things but also implies reliability and solidity. Blue is the color of the sky, but it's also considered restful and soothing, and in most polls on the subject, a majority of people choose it as their favorite color. Red is passionate and arousing, while pink, created by adding white to red, is calming. Orange is also stimulating (witness its use in many fast-food restaurants), but its pastel versions, such as peach and terra-cotta, are more relaxed.

Think about the emotions and feeling you want to create in each room. For example, a soothing blue or pink might be best in the bedroom, with a stimulating red in the dining room, a calming green in the living room, and an energetic yellow in the kitchen.

COMBINING COLORS

Choosing the colors you'd like to use in a decorating scheme is one challenge; putting them together is another. Creating a color scheme can be tricky. Sometimes color combinations just fall into place (after all, we're not talking nuclear physics here), but interior decorating involves a lot of decisions and time and money. You want the results to be pleasing enough to last, so it's crucial to spend some time on getting it right.

How many colors can you use? The conventional wisdom is that the large surfaces of a room (walls, ceiling, floor, window treatments) should be restricted to no more than three dominant colors (it's all right to use a print with more than three colors if only one or two prevail). Otherwise there is no real limit, except that of personal taste, to the number of accent colors you can use on pillows, accessories, flowers, and the like. Think of the myriad colors in an Oriental rug and you'll understand how seemingly unrelated hues can work beautifully together. You may find that chance plays a part, just as you may discover that certain items of clothing go together by accidentally juxtaposing them in the laundry bag.

Don't worry about matching colors exactly. A too-perfect match gives a room a stiff, formal feeling—an effect that decorators often refer to disparagingly as "matchy-matchy." Presumably you want to achieve an effect that is sophisticated but relaxed. After all, in the natural world, many subtle variations of colors exist quite happily together without matching, and we are all the better for it.

There are several ways to create an effective and pleasing balance of colors in a room. One approach is to keep most of the room in shades of a single color (such as blue), a balance in a harmonious second color (green), and a few objects in a completely contrasting color as accents (perhaps red or orange). Another choice is to make everything one color and add interest with texture—a difficult scheme to get right, since there is a fine line between restful and dull. A third possibility is to use a single hue overall and combine it with a single, sparingly used accent color (such as a white room with blue accents).

Traditional decorating schemes usually put the darkest tones on the floor, medium tones on the walls, and light tones on the ceiling. However, this is not a hard-and-fast rule. Generally, window treatments and upholstery should contrast somewhat with walls to keep everything from blending together and becoming too bland. Variations on medium tones are usually suggested. Use neutral tones in large areas and bright, intense colors in smaller areas and for accessories.

Planning a color scheme for a whole house or apartment is an extension of planning for a single room. It's more complicated, of course, since you need to think about the flow from one area to another. A large house with well-defined, separated rooms is easier to plan than a small house or apartment. For a smaller space you have to think about creating a harmonious whole. It makes sense to envision an overall palette of colors that work well together and can be used in various proportions from room to room. Each room will seem different, but the effect of the whole will be of a pleasant overall scheme at work.

Open plans with adjoining rooms also affect a color scheme. Since one room is clearly visible from the next, each must be compatible with the other. Let color flow through the house, and use textures and proportions to keep the effect from getting monotonous. Manufacturers have tried to make this task easy by creating suites of coordinated wallcoverings and fabrics, but you can also do it on your own, which allows for greater individual creativity.

What's outside the windows counts too. In a top-floor apartment you'll have natural light and views of a changing sky or the tops of trees. In a suburban home the windows will look out on a garden, lawn, or, if you're lucky, woods, which you may want to relate to your interior by means of color. Keep in mind that every landscape has a number of color palettes related to the seasons.

One way of making final decisions about a color scheme is to assemble scraps and samples of each fabric, material, pattern, and color you plan to use and put them together. Make the sample proportionate in size to its anticipated use in the room. This will give you a better feeling for how intense a color, for example, you want to use in a large area. Professional decorators make a "color board," applying paint samples and fabric and carpet swatches to a drawing (also known as an elevation) of the room. If you have some drawing ability, you can create your own color board. Make a drawing of the room and paint or color in the colors to get an idea of how the scheme will look.

For those who feel they can't draw well enough, a tabletop will do just as well. Lay out your color swatches, then step back and take a careful, considered look. You can even try narrowing your eyes and squinting at the ensemble to get an overall, swift impression, as suggested by decorators Emily Malino and Mary

USING THE COLOR WHEEL

The color wheel (following page 112) portrays the relationships among the three primary colors (red, blue, yellow); the three secondary colors that result from mixing two primary colors (purple, green, orange); and the tertiary colors made by mixing a primary with a secondary color (for example, yellow-green, red-orange, and blue-violet). All colors, with the exception of the primary colors, are made from other colors. Mixing pure hues with white and black can create hundreds of different tints and shades.

Like any other field of study, color has its own vocabulary. *Complementary colors*, or *complements*, are those directly opposite each other on the color wheel, such as blue and orange or red and green. *Analogous colors* are those next to each other on the color wheel. *Value* refers to the lightness or darkness of a single hue. Color values affect each other when placed side by side; a lighter value will make a darker one seem darker, and vice versa. *Hues* are pure colors except for black, white, and gray. *Shades* are hues with black added, darkening them, while *tints* are hues with white added. *Tones* are hues with gray added. *Intensity* is used to describe the brightness or dullness of a color. To change the intensity of a color from the most intense (the pure hue), either black or white is added. But for a richer color, some of the hue's complement is added.

The color wheel can be used to develop color schemes. Related, or analogous, color schemes usually combine three neighboring colors from the color wheel. Complementary color schemes use two colors opposite each other on the color wheel. Triadic schemes are based on three colors equally spaced around the color wheel, such as red, yellow, and blue; yellow-green, blue-violet, and red-orange; or orange, green, and violet.

Analogous schemes can be warm or cool, since the colors are adjacent on the color wheel and therefore usually share these attributes. Complementary schemes are bold and often intriguing. They can be difficult to pull off because the contrasts are bold and placing them side by side makes them seem more intense, but they can be effective if done properly. According to color theory developed at the Bauhaus, an influential government design school that flourished in 1920s Germany, mixing complementary colors relaxes the eye because the colors move toward gray. Triadic schemes tend to be the most sophisticated, since the relationships among the colors are the most abstract. Experiment with intensity and values in a triadic color scheme for the best results. A red, yellow, and blue scheme with all colors of the same intensity might seem too bright, but deep red and navy blue with pale yellow or deep gold used as an accent is another story.

Gilliatt. This way you'll be able to see quickly which colors and textures work together and which ones do not work or detract from the whole.

Another method is to shoot an overexposed black-and-white photograph of each wall in a room. Blow it up to eight by ten inches, make a series of light photocopies, and then color them with colored pencils to try different schemes.

Still another variation is to make a chart representing the proportions of the ceiling, floor, walls, window treatments, upholstery, and accents and then color it in order to get a visual approximation of how the colors work together. In the illustration in the color insert, the walls and floor are neutral tones (ivory and wood tone), the upholstered furniture is covered in mellow golds sparked with accents of turquoise and red, and neutrals—pure white, black, and gray—are used for furniture frames and other details.

INCORPORATING PATTERNS AND TEXTURES

Patterns and textures serve an important function in decorating. They add liveliness and sparkle to a color scheme and can effectively spice up a room that seems flat and unexciting. Your choice of patterns will be guided by style of decoration—whether modern, traditional, or country—the requirements of the room, and your personal preferences.

Selecting appropriate patterns for fabrics and wallpaper can seem daunting, particularly when you have to match them to furniture, carpeting, wallpaper, or other existing features not being replaced. There are so many possibilities to choose from—traditional prints in subdued tones, brightly colored abstracts, pastel miniprints with coordinating borders—that it's difficult to know where to begin.

Begin by evaluating the needs of the room. Pattern, like color, can be used to affect proportions. There are a few rules of thumb. Complex patterns using several colors and broken, criss-crossing, or diagonal lines are "busy" to the eye and can make a long stretch of wall seem less dull and a large room more intimate. Conversely, a small room might be overwhelmed by such a pattern.

Vertical lines can make a high-ceilinged room seem too tall, but a room with a low ceiling will benefit from a sense of height. Horizontal stripes, for some reason, seem more soothing and restful, subdued and tranquil, and they lend a sense of space. Although large patterns are often out of scale in a small room, sometimes they can give a sense of grandeur or drama.

Think of the size and scale of your pattern in relation to the area it will cover. In general, the bigger the area, the larger the pattern, but it can be effective and fun to play with the scale and put a large print on a small piece of furniture and vice versa.

The same pattern or group of related patterns used throughout an area creates a sense of flow and continuity. The use of related patterns can give a group of rooms—such as the living, dining, and family areas—a sense of subtle differentiation without seeming too divisive. The same holds true for the "great rooms" seen in many contemporary homes.

How a print or pattern is colored also affects how it is perceived. Colors close in value, rather than high in contrast, seem more subdued and restful. A strong contrast of colors will make the same print seem much livelier.

Texture also affects colors and your perception of them in various ways. Rough, nubby textures absorb light, while smooth textures reflect it. Rough, loosely woven textures tend to increase the apparent size and height of an object, while smooth, satiny weaves reflect light and almost seem to "dematerialize" the object they cover. Earth tones and coarse textures are practical and hide dirt but also can be dreary. Look for soil-resistant finishes on fabrics and rugs if you want to use light or bright tones. Dark colors can also be subject to soiling, and black doesn't hide dust.

Richly textured materials in full-bodied jewel tones give a formal feeling—think of Oriental and Persian rugs, brocades, damasks, and silk jacquards. On the other hand, lighter colors and smoother weaves, such as pastel printed cottons and glazed chintzes, are definitely more informal and are a strong component of country styles.

Select a pattern that appeals to you and works well in your overall scheme. The best approach, once again, is to collect samples of carpets, wall coverings, and upholstery and curtain fabrics (working with a decorator makes this easy) and from this group select the patterns and textures that seem to work well together. Don't be afraid to experiment, especially with smaller items such as throw pillows, tablecloths, and napkins. If you have selected a basically neutral color scheme, these details will help to liven it up and give it a sense of style.

EXERCISES

The following color exercises should give you plenty of visual material to help you decide on a new color scheme for your home.

1. Look carefully at a painting, antique textile, vase of flowers, or other object that successfully combines colors you really like and write down all of the colors that make it up. Try to estimate the proportions and different shades that go into the overall effect.

2. Think of your favorite color and your emotional response to it. Think of the different tones that might be inherent in the same shade and all of the things, real or fanciful, the color reminds you of. Try this mental exercise with other hues, even those you like but aren't sure you want to include.

3. Gather together your favorite color photographs, postcards, clippings from magazines, posters, fabric scraps, and other objects. You probably will discover that a single color or combination of colors predominates, creating an instant guide to your preferences. Make a list of the colors you find most often.

4. What kind of natural light does each room you are decorating receive? Under what lighting conditions will each room most often be seen? Make a room-by-room list, noting the types of light.

5. Use crayons, watercolors, colored paper, paint, or natural objects (pebbles, flowers, leaves, vegetables, fruit) to experiment with color combinations. Try anything. Record the combinations you like best.

6. Imagine how you might use your favorite color in various schemes. Here's an example using blue:

   Monochromatic: blue with tints and shades of blue
   Analogous: blue with blue-violet and blue-green
   Complementary: blue with orange (for example, this scheme may translate into terra-cotta with green patina or aqua, or peachy shades with grayed blue)
   Triadic: blue with yellow and red, or a variation such as blue-violet with red-orange and yellow-green

   Neutrals particularly black, white, and gray, can be used to set off any of these schemes.

Note the combinations of your favorite colors, along with ideas for how you might use them in a particular room. Think of these exercises as your "color play," rather than a lineup of deadly serious activities. The idea is to help you get acquainted with the qualities inherent in and associated with your favorite colors and to keep you from getting bogged down by details. In the world of nature, colors are wonderful and sensuous, delightful to the eye. Creating a good color scheme, one that suits both you and your home, should be fun, not work. Approach it in the spirit of adventure.

3

CHOOSING A STYLE

What, exactly, is "style"? In the context of interior decorating, style has two definitions, one broad and sweeping and the other much more specific. In a general sense, style is very personal, a way of choosing colors and shapes and objects and textures and putting them together. The other meaning of style is easier to define: the identifying characteristics of a particular country, region, or era, or sometimes all three. These include national and regional styles, such as English country, Caribbean, and Southwestern, and styles identified with a historical period, such as Regency, Arts and Crafts, colonial, and Victorian. Even historical styles have a more general meaning, referring to shape and motif rather than to a specific era; terms such as *baroque*, *rococo*, and *neoclassical* refer both to the styles of certain periods and to their later revivals and reinterpretations. There are also styles named for furniture designers and design schools, such as Chippendale and Bauhaus, as well as the styles of this century—art nouveau (1890–1918), art deco (1918–1939), art moderne (1930–1939), and high tech, minimalism, and postmodern (styles that began in the 1970s).

This plethora of styles can seem overwhelming when you're trying to choose one for your home, a task that is even more intimidating than selecting a color scheme. The usual advice is to find the style that suits you best and stick with it, but how do you do that?

FINDING A STYLE

As with selecting colors, there are certain straightforward steps to take in selecting a style. You must really look at shapes and motifs carefully and be analytical about what you like. Get out your collection of clippings and this time think about the shapes and styles that appeal to you. Analyze what you like most about a particular room setting or piece of furniture or window treatment. Concentrate on styles and shapes rather than color, which is irrelevant here.

Probably the best way to choose a country or regional style is to visit a bookstore or library and study the shelves of trendy "style" books, such as *Santa Fe Style*, *American Country*, *French Country*, and similar titles (see the Bibliography at the end of the book for suggested titles). If you find a book that is especially appealing to you, and you think it would be helpful, you might want to buy a copy for reference. For historic styles look carefully at the period rooms in historic houses and museums.

You can even use videos and television as a source of information. Check out the video of a favorite film and see if you'd like to translate any of the sets into a room of your own. Romantic comedies of the 1930s, for example, are great sources for art deco effects. Examine the mood and feeling created by the film to discover if any of the elements might be adapted to complement the interior of your home.

Of course, you may already have a starting point if your house or apartment has a distinctive style of its own. This doesn't mean you have to follow a strict style in decorating or that you can't mix in things from other styles, but it does mean that you should have respect for the existing walls and mortar. A snug Cape Cod cottage would look silly done up like Versailles, while casual American country or high-tech minimalism wouldn't exactly suit a Georgian-style mansion. An old farmhouse looks best filled with country pieces, and a beach or summer house should be relaxed, as suits its use.

Even if your home lacks distinctive architectural details, the physical aspects of the rooms can influence a choice of style. If a room is light and airy, you can exploit that by emphasizing these qualities—choosing bright or pale colors and slender, spare, unobtrusive furniture—or you can take the opportunity to use heavy furniture and dark colors without worrying that the room will turn into a claustrophobic closet. The same idea holds true of a dark, rather snug room. You can make it cozy with dark, warm colors and soothing textures or use light colors, reflective surfaces, and concealed lighting to brighten it up. If a room is boxy and seemingly without character, you can apply moldings and use decorative paint techniques to jazz it up and give it an identity. Whatever a room is like, you can use its character as a clue to what might be done with it.

Of course, you may already have a decorating style you love and don't want to change. You may have a collection of Mexican folk art or vintage English teapots or a magnificent Victorian dining table. Then it's a question of fitting your own style to that of the house or the room without violating either one. Use the methods suggested above—explore your clipping file, study historic rooms, adapt the existing architectural style of your home—to get started.

COUNTRY STYLES

Whatever their provenance, country styles have rustic charm. The basic elements of a country style include mellow woods such as pine and oak, painted and stained furniture, wall tiles, handwoven rugs, stoneware, china figures, engravings, embroidery, and patchwork. Country furniture and furnishings cover a broad spectrum, from genuine farmhouse antiques to contemporary pieces done in a country style using the appropriate materials.

Country style is relatively inexpensive and appeals to many people. It has the allure of the handcrafted and the unpretentious. None of this furniture is at all grand, nor is it meant to be. Country pieces are versatile. The shapes and materials are usually simple enough that they mix well with other styles, adding charm and a sense of the past without aggressively taking things over. They supply a sense of individuality and can really "make" a room. Warm and idiosyncratic, country pieces generally work well with other styles, from neoclassical to modern.

English Country

The term *country style* covers a lot of ground. English country, for example, is pretty and fresh, relaxed, elegant, and conveys a slight sense of disarray. Colors are warm but slightly faded blues, greens, and reds. It generally features somewhat timeworn slipcovers, often of flowered chintz, and slightly worn Oriental or Persian rugs over wood floors or sisal matting. White plaster walls and old pine furniture, casual flower arrangements displayed in pretty bits of china, and lots of casual throws for the sofas are typical. Several loose pillows in needlepoint or tapestry add to the effect.

French Country

French country is more Mediterranean, featuring a choice of charming Provençal prints in rich, intense reds and blues, blue- and red-checked fabrics, or faded toiles printed with scenes of country life in pink or blue. Floors are most often of terra-cotta tile covered with straw mats. Furniture is made of chestnut or pine, and chairs have caned seats and curved legs.

American Country

American country offers primitive eighteenth-century furniture, faded reds and blues, plain, bare floorboards covered with braided rugs, and wooden beds draped with patchwork quilts. Small prints and checks are typical fabrics, and stenciled walls and painted floorcloths may add to the charm. Rocking chairs, Windsor-style settees, four-poster beds, and the refined, yet very simple and clean, lines of Shaker furniture are among the most popular types of furnishings.

American Southwest

The American Southwest style reflects the influence of Spanish and Native American cultures on the basically northern European roots of early American style. Southwestern interiors display rough-hewn furniture, Navajo rugs, Hopi and Anasazi pottery, straw matting, and the use of bright colors and oversized elements—large-scale patterns, high-back chairs, and giant decorative accessories—often combined with black, in distinctive patterns inspired by Native American textiles.

Mediterranean Country

Mediterranean country styles—those of Italy, Greece, Turkey, North Africa, and southern Spain—reflect the constant presence of strong sunlight in those climates and emphasize thick walls, usually of stone or plaster, with deep niches for windows, and shielded by louvered window shutters. The furniture is simple in design and often made of wood and cane. Upholstered furniture may be covered in white linen trimmed with lace. Pierced wooden screens provide further sun protection.

Scandinavian Country

Scandinavian style is typified by painted wood furniture, bare floorboards, cool, clear colors, and crisp blue-and-white checks, seen most often on fabric but also in painted or tiled motifs. The effect is both soothing and stimulating, well suited to contemporary life.

PERIOD STYLES

The use of period styles seldom entails a slavish, scholarly re-creation but rather employs traditional motifs, forms, and colors. Nostalgia plays a part as well. The past seems warm, cozy, and inviting, whatever its style—and sometimes the present seems so bleak that we're happy to escape into another time (with modern conveniences close at hand, of course). As an introduction, some of the most popular period styles are described in the following sections. For more information on a particular period, you may want to consult the style books recommended in the Bibliography.

GEORGIAN AND COLONIAL

The mid-eighteenth century was the beginning of the Georgian period in England and the colonial period in the United States. Known as the age of elegance for good reason, it is probably the most popular period of decorating style today. Designs are simple and use classical motifs, but materials are rich, including figured silk, mahogany, and silver. Window treatments tend to be uncomplicated, usually featuring simple festoon curtains in unlined silk with a valance trimmed in braid. Drop-front writing desks, wooden dining chairs with carved and pierced splat backs, and pedestal side tables are popular Georgian furniture types that are available today in affordable reproductions.

Also typical of the mid-Georgian period are Gothic (or, in England, "Gothick") motifs, including pointed arches and elaborate tracery, and chinoiserie—Oriental motifs and materials found in porcelain, lacquer work, faux bamboo, and such vivid color combinations as brilliant scarlet red or emerald green contrasted with black and gilt. Late Georgian design shows the influence of Robert Adam, the great English neoclassical architect, and is far more severe and scholarly in its use of classical motifs. Satinwood joins mahogany as the most popular wood used in furniture making. Fabrics and colors are much more subdued in pattern than in earlier eras.

Regency and Federal

Regency style dominated in the early nineteenth century in England, and a similar style in the United States is known as Federal. Walls are divided into the classic tripartite mode of dado or wainscoting, field, and frieze. Patterned wallpapers or painted walls with stenciled trim in a Greek key or anthemion (honeysuckle) motif are typical, as are strong colors in sophisticated combinations, such as lilac with yellow, emerald with crimson, and deep pinks and blues. Fitted wall-to-wall carpeting began to be used in the wealthiest homes, and rich fabrics—watered and moiré silks, brocades, and damasks—were used to create elaborate asymmetrical curtains festooned with fringe and tassels and adorned with decorative hardware such as brackets, finials, rings, rosettes, and tiebacks. Important furniture types include single- and double-ended couches in the styles known as recamier or *meridienne*, also called Grecian couches, and saber-legged dining chairs in mahogany, lacquer, or ebonized wood trimmed in gilt.

Biedermeier

Austrian and German early-nineteenth-century neoclassical Biedermeier furniture, typified by its mix of light and dark woods and simple classical motifs, enjoyed great popularity among the discerning middle classes then and continues to be popular today. Most Biedermeier pieces are simple in form and mix well with furniture of other styles as well as a variety of color schemes. Genuine Biedermeier pieces are rare and expensive, but some reproductions are available today for relatively affordable prices.

Victorian

The rest of the nineteenth century was diverse and fragmented. Early Victorian style incorporated a taste for rosewood, plump scrolled arms, and curved backs on dining chairs. Monumental sofas with overstuffed cushions and fringed and tasseled bolsters provided a place to recline, while around the massive round pedestal-base table in the library, one could catch up on recent events in the newspaper.

High Victorian interiors were distinguished by bands of stenciled architectural ornament, now available as preprinted wallpaper borders. Furniture remained massive. Lace curtains, hung up against the glass to diffuse sunlight, became popular. There were fads for Greek and Egyptian styles, another Gothic revival, and the japonaiserie style of the aesthetic movement. Within this diversity, nineteenth-century styles feature solid construction and attention to detail. The use of fringe, tassels, deep, rich colors, and a mix of many patterns contribute to the overall look.

Arts and Crafts

In the 1890s, when the elaborate Victorian styles were beginning to wane in popularity, a simpler look came to the fore—the Arts and Crafts style. Also known as mission, craftsman, or craftsman modern (to avoid confusing it with the British style of the same name but different origins), it is characterized by the use of homespun fabrics, austere shapes, clean, muted colors, and natural materials, such as stone, brick, glazed tile, copper, bronze, and dark-tone woods, particularly oak. In style Arts and Crafts furniture is distinctive, featuring simple, rectilinear lines and massive proportions. Typically pieces are made of oak, often fumed to make the wood darker. They are ornamented with simple geometric cutouts and copper or bronze hardware. Fabrics of the period also have distinctive patterns, usually of small-scale, stylized flowers and leaves in soft, pale hues, especially muted greens, blues, and browns. The geometric motifs and general plainness and restraint of the Arts and Crafts style make it the precursor to many modern styles of the twentieth century.

Modern

There are many versions of the modern style, from the purist chromed-steel-and-glass interpretation of the 1920s to the biomorphic, sometimes kitsch American modernism of the 1940s and 1950s. Other early modern styles include sinuous art nouveau, geometric art deco, and luxurious art moderne.

Art nouveau reached its height of popularity around the turn of the century and continued as a recognized style until the First World War. Also known as *Jugendstil* in Germany, *stilo nuovo* in Italy, and Liberty (after the department store) in England, it combines austere elegance with curvilinear, flowing motifs of long-stemmed, stylized flowers and abstract birds. Typical of the style are richly stenciled borders and hand-printed wallpapers in deep pastels, including pink, lilac, yellow, and pale green. Furniture tends to be simple, with strong, unfussy silhouettes and striking cut-out motifs of hearts or crescents. One of the best-known practitioners of the style was Glasgow architect Charles Rennie Mackintosh, whose bold black-and-white lacquered furniture, often upholstered in jewel tones, is now available in reproduction. His fondness for grid and checkerboard patterns foreshadowed art deco.

Art deco and art moderne are styles typical of the 1920s and 1930s. While classic Bauhaus modernism, which originated in the 1920s in Germany, relied on industrial styles and such materials as chromed steel, plate glass, plastics, and rubber, deco and moderne designs incorporated influences from popular and commercial culture. The art deco movement is characterized by the innovative uses of textiles, ceramics, and metalwork in furniture and decorative objects. Furniture tends to be geometric in form, incorporating strict angles or curvilinear motifs with clean lines and smooth planes. The deep colors typical of the style—ultramarine, lilac, and various reds—are often accented with black and silver (sometimes gold). Fabrics combine geometric motifs, especially prisms or stepped pyramids, with floral or other naturalistic figures in bright colors. Upholstered furniture tends to be plump, with broad, flat arms. Double-tiered tables with glass shelves serve to display the decorative objects and necessities peculiar to the period, including cigarette boxes, cocktail shakers, and large marble or ceramic ashtrays.

Art moderne furniture and accessories adapt some of art deco's motifs. The style differs from art deco mainly in terms of colors, using a monochromatic palette generally restricted to black, shades of cream, and white. Moderne pieces sport a sophisticated, streamlined silhouette with an emphasis on chrome and glass. The overall look is horizontal rather than vertical, with long, low sofas often upholstered in white or cream. Equally low-slung chrome-and-glass tables and mirrored screens are used as background. Bleached and pickled woods, along with shaggy-pile white rugs, are typical of the look.

Furniture and accessories in the mainstream modern style, invented in the mid-1920s but not really popular until the 1930s, 1940s, and 1950s, employ industrial materials (chromed or painted steel, plate glass, plastics) and processes (laminated and bent wood, industrial coatings such as epoxy enamel on metal). As contrast to these sleek materials, the preferred upholstery styles are of leather or pony skin or coarsely woven, nubby-textured fabrics in earth tones (the nubby textures are more typical of the 1950s). Furniture design is characterized by a lack of obviously decorative details and instead uses either straight, rectilinear shapes or abstracted, biomorphic curves.

Modern furniture designs by European masters of the 1920s and 1930s, such as Alvar Aalto, Mies van der Rohe, Le Corbusier, and Marcel Breuer, are widely available in reproduction, as are the designs of American geniuses Charles Eames, Harry Bertoia, and Eero Saarinen, whose best-known work appeared in the 1940s and 1950s. Modern pieces can also be discovered at flea markets, auction houses, and estate sales at fairly reasonable prices. Modern designs mix well with other simple, clean-lined furniture and sometimes work as a contrast to a single highly ornate piece.

Contemporary

High-tech interiors, at the height of their popularity in the mid- to late 1970s, are stripped down and minimalist, using off-the-shelf industrial materials such as steel shelving and commercial carpeting. Although pure high-tech interiors seem dated now, some of their elements, such as clean lines, everyday materials used in imaginative ways, and a limited palette of soft colors, can be combined successfully with other styles.

Postmodernism, as typified by Italian and American furniture of the 1980s, employs modified classical motifs and modern materials and sometimes jokingly refers to earlier eras, from the nineteenth century to the 1950s. For example, Robert Venturi's chairs for Knoll, made of brightly painted, laminated, bent plywood, have backs that are cut out to resemble flat, almost cartoonish versions of such historical styles as Chippendale, Regency, and art deco. Michael Graves takes the opposite tack with his elegant art deco– or Biedermeier-esque furniture using bird's-eye maple and ebony. Memphis furniture, designed by a group of Italian architects (the most famous of whom is Ettore Sottsass), perhaps defines the postmodern style. With an emphasis on laminates and veneers, Memphis furniture uses a variety of materials and a mixture of styles, from deco to fifties rec room—often all in the same piece. While the height of post-modernism has passed, and many of the designs from the era seem overly slick or ironic now, the lesson learned from the eclectic mixing of the period can be applied to creating relaxed yet sophisticated rooms to suit today's comfortable lifestyles.

ECLECTIC STYLE

An eclectic approach to interior decorating happens naturally. Most people find that they have wide-ranging tastes. They own objects in a variety of styles but don't know how to put them together in a harmonious scheme. In addition, people living together in a household often have dissimilar tastes, and a successful decorative scheme needs to accommodate their differences.

The solution to such situations is an eclectic scheme that combines various styles. Mixing gives you the chance to use your imagination and really put your taste to work. After all, if you're not careful, a purist period room can be predictable and boring. There are only so many good antique pieces around, and originals and high-quality reproductions are expensive. You probably will have to improvise in any case. So, why not make improvisation the whole point of the exercise?

Eclecticism, if done well and handled correctly, can create wonderful rooms that are exciting to be in, both for those who live in them and for those encountering them for the first time. They can be exhilarating and inspiring or calm and soothing, but they are always wonderful. A talent for mixing periods and styles is what most famous decorators have based their careers on. You can mix furnishings from various periods, or modern furniture with classical and neoclassical accessories, or folk art with country furniture. Some mixtures are more obvious than others; some may surprise you with how well they work. Successful eclecticism depends on a strong sense of form, scale, and color, a willingness to take chances and experiment, a sense of humor, and self-confidence. It doesn't require a great deal of money.

However diverse the elements are, there should be a single factor that unites them. Color is one good choice. For example, you could take a selection of very different wood dining chairs and paint them all glossy white. Wall-to-wall carpeting or a room-size rug can have the same effect, providing a background that ties everything together. An overall white or cream-tone scheme also serves as an excellent way to show off a varied group of furnishings and accessories. Eclectic schemes are good settings for a collection of exotic Asian or African folk art pieces, Latin American santos, or Amish quilts. Imagination and a willingness to experiment are the keys to a successful eclectic decorating scheme.

EXERCISES

1. Make a list of styles that appeal to you. Is there a particular period in history that you especially like?

____

____

____

____

____

____

____

____

____

____

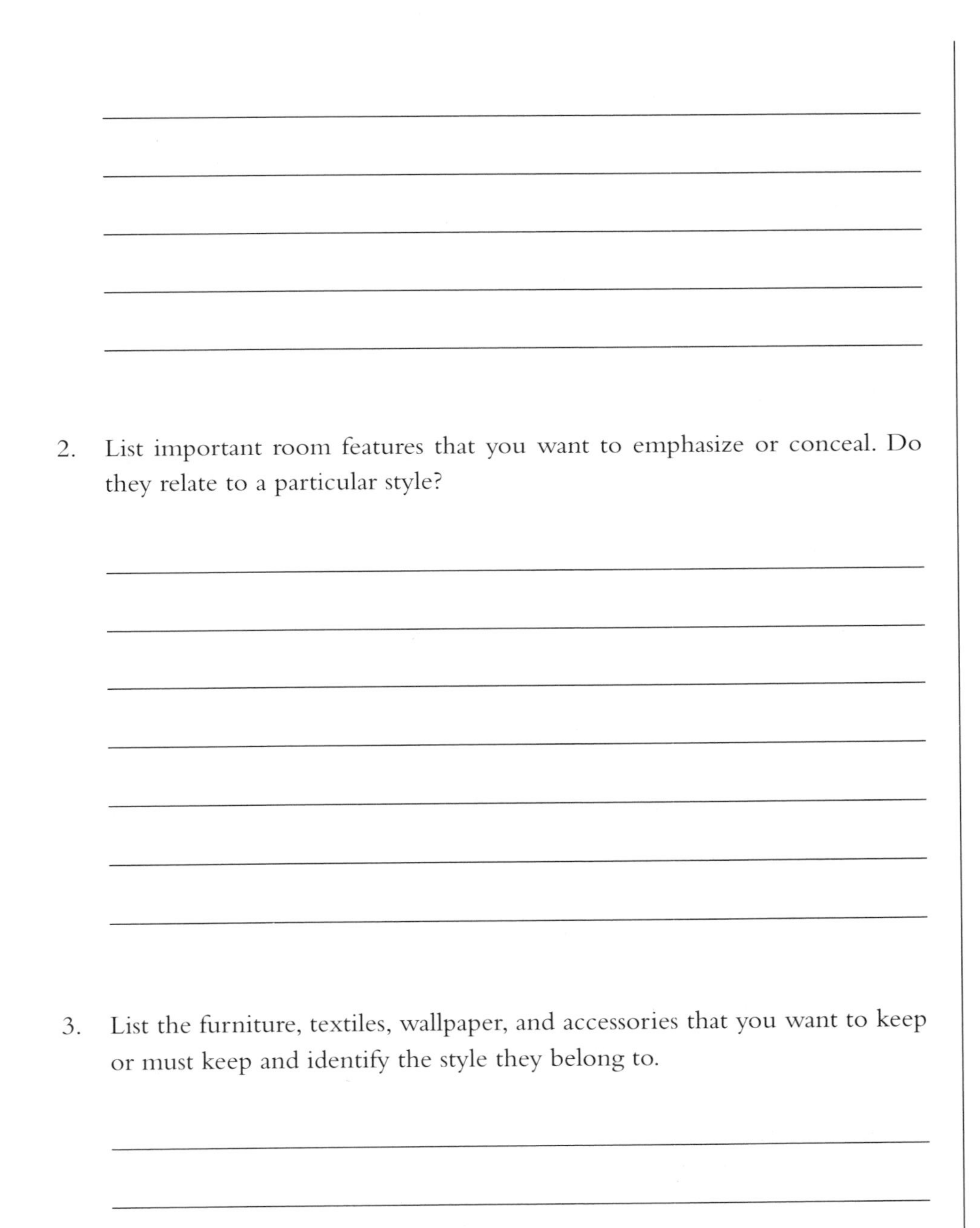

2. List important room features that you want to emphasize or conceal. Do they relate to a particular style?

3. List the furniture, textiles, wallpaper, and accessories that you want to keep or must keep and identify the style they belong to.

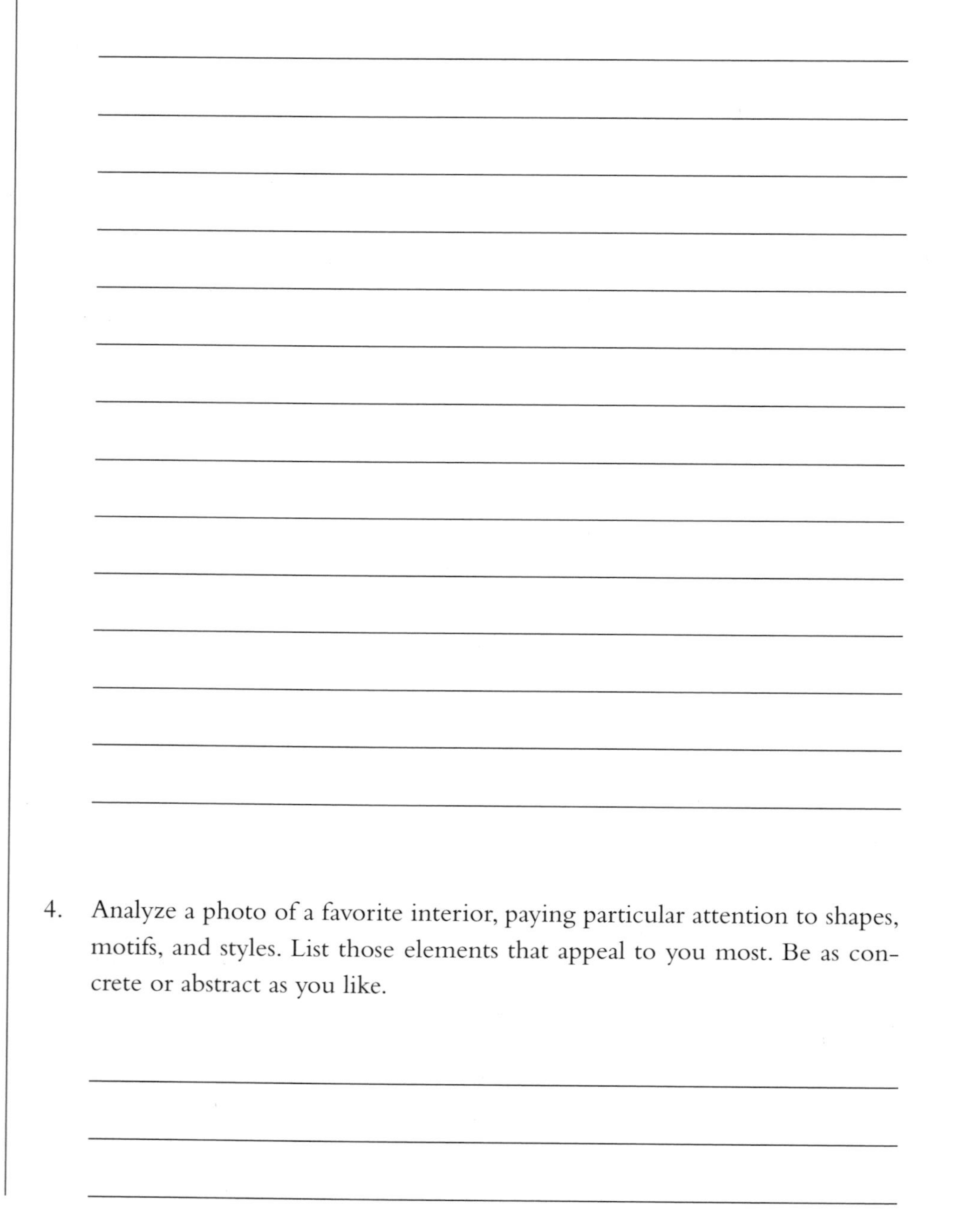

4. Analyze a photo of a favorite interior, paying particular attention to shapes, motifs, and styles. List those elements that appeal to you most. Be as concrete or abstract as you like.

5. Do you prefer formal or informal styles? You may want to vary the style you choose from room to room, depending on function and atmosphere. List the possibilities below:

Room	*Style Possibilities*

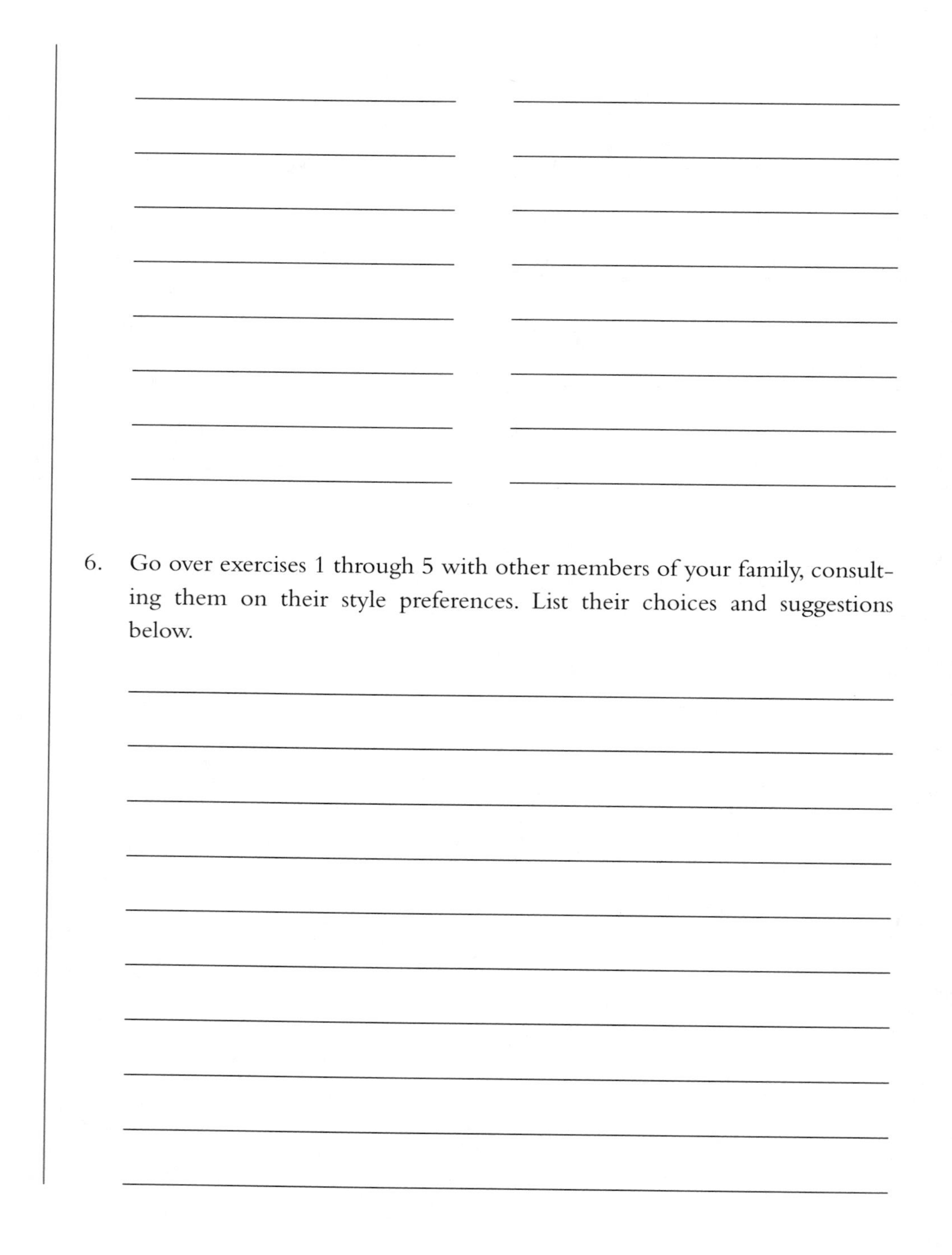

6. Go over exercises 1 through 5 with other members of your family, consulting them on their style preferences. List their choices and suggestions below.

Once you have completed the exercises in the first three chapters, you should have a fairly clear idea of your general intentions in terms of overall decorating plan, color scheme, and style. The next step is to adapt this overall plan to specific rooms. This process is discussed in the next several chapters, room by room.

The choice as to the best way of using this handbook is up to you. If you are redoing an entire house, you may want to go through each chapter, taking notes along the way. If you are really only interested in putting up some new window treatments or replacing your carpeting, by all means skip ahead to the chapters that deal specifically with those topics. And if you want to redecorate a single room, consult the relevant chapter as well as the chapters dealing with specific topics such as walls, floors, lighting, and windows, and you should have all the information you need to complete your redecorating project successfully.

PART TWO

✦ ✦ ✦ ✦

YOUR HOME, ROOM BY ROOM

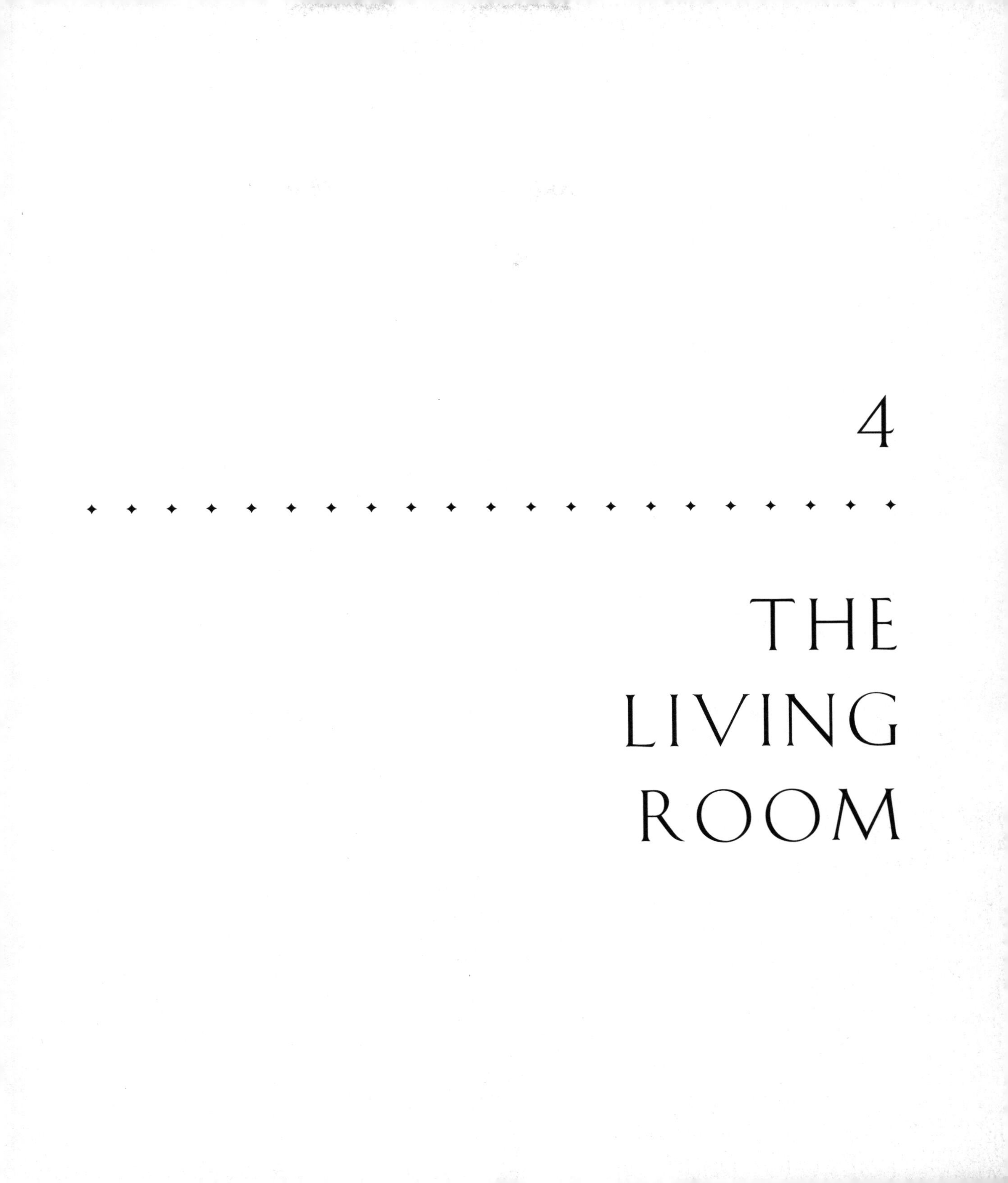

4

THE LIVING ROOM

Your living room is a place where your family and guests spend a lot of time. It also serves a symbolic function as the keynote of your home. It is a room that must be on show, on its best behavior, but for many people it must also be a very practical room that serves multiple functions, from study and playroom to music room, TV room, and dining room.

You may be fortunate enough to have a separate playroom (discussed in Chapter 12) or family room (Chapter 8) and thus be able to maintain an elegant living room for formal occasions. But not many of us can afford to have a room we hardly ever use. As entertaining and socializing become more informal, the formal living room is becoming an anachronism. Besides, with the proper materials, finishes, and enough storage, a casual leave-the-toys-out, put-the-feet-up sort of space can be transformed into a place of elegance within minutes.

To plan a living room that fits your particular living situation, you should follow the process described in Chapter 1 for creating a decorating scheme. First, you will need to create a master file of clippings and samples and draw a floor plan of the living room. Then, using the exercises at the end of Chapter 1, you can evaluate the existing conditions, work out a budget, and plan a schedule. If you have trouble deciding on a new color scheme for your living room, you'll

CHECKLIST

1. Is the traffic pattern through the room convenient and satisfactory?
2. Do you have enough seating for your entertainment needs?
3. Do you have enough storage to get clutter out of the way quickly and easily?
4. Is your seating area arranged around a focal point?
5. Have you established a color scheme?
6. Have you thought about what furniture you need to buy?
7. Have you considered reusing existing furniture?
8. Have you made a floor plan of the room?

benefit by following the guidelines in Chapter 2. For information on styles of decoration, from Regency to postmodern, country to eclectic, refer to Chapter 3. This chapter is designed to help you handle problems specific to the living room.

SOFAS, CHAIRS, AND TABLES

Furniture placement in a room designed for entertainment and togetherness should center around a focal point. It might be a working fireplace or a well-designed entertainment center or a beautiful view. Once you've chosen the focal point, group the furniture around it, using enough pieces to be flexible.

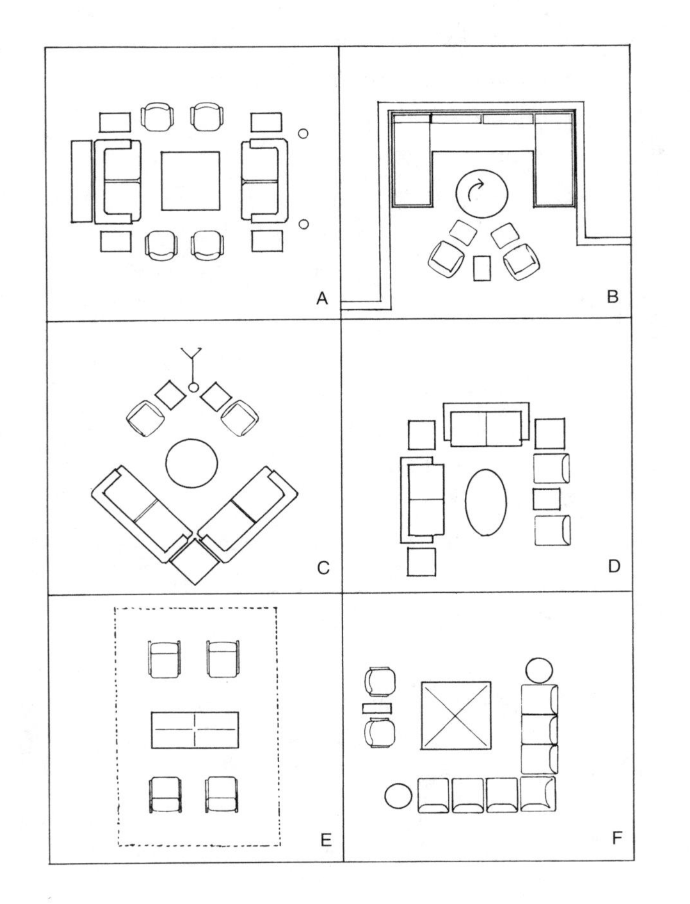

Seating Arrangements

A. *The console behind the sofa serves as a desk. It also could be a a nice spot to display art and current reading material.*

B. *A U-shaped arrangement of upholstered foam mattresses on plywood platforms with matching bolsters creates an alcove for reading and napping.*

C. *Placing furniture on a diagonal adds dynamic energy to a grouping and can make a small room seem larger.*

D. *Every seat in this group is next to a surface for a lamp, a book, or a drink.*

E. *An arrangement like this one works well in a small room, but it can be somewhat formal.*

F. *The large coffee table brings the oversize sectional sofa into scale with the smaller armchairs.*

A very small space might take only a sofa and an armchair plus small occasional tables, while a bigger space might accommodate a large sofa, two chairs, a coffee table, end tables, and even more pieces.

Sofas and large armchairs are anchor pieces. They serve both to establish the style of a room and to supply comfortable seating. Upholstered pieces are available in a wide variety of shapes and sizes, from historical to ultramodern. Whatever your style choice, try in general to seat six comfortably and keep extra seating, such as folding chairs or even large floor pillows, stashed away to accommodate larger gatherings. Or plan to bring in chairs from other rooms. Conventional seating arrangements generally include one or two sofas, armchairs, and occasional chairs. In a small room you might omit the sofa and instead have two or three very comfortable armchairs, perhaps spaced around a low coffee table. An alternative might be a loveseat and an armchair. Furniture should be versatile enough to be rearranged for various situations.

Side, occasional, and coffee tables are also important elements in a living room. They come in a variety of materials and styles, from all types of wood to metal and glass and shiny, elegant lacquer. Glass-top tables have the advantage of being easy to clean. They also take up less visual space and therefore work well in small rooms. Because of their transparency, they work especially well over ornamental carpets. If you don't have room for a coffee table, you can use nesting tables. The top table of the set can be used to hold a lamp or bric-a-brac, while the lower two can slide out to hold coffee cups or glasses. In a large room you might want to put a table or console behind the sofa (it should be the same height as the sofa back) as well as a coffee table in front and individual side tables for other seating pieces.

Furniture arrangement should reflect activity areas. A small room should have at least a single conversational grouping. In a larger room you can have additional furniture groupings to reflect other activities, such as reading, watching television, or even writing letters at a desk. (See Chapter 8, "The Family Room," for further discussion of activity areas.)

It isn't necessary to buy all new furniture when you decorate. If the existing upholstery is too good to change, or you can't afford to change it but feel the need for something new, you have various options. If the upholstery is plain, add patterned throw pillows in harmonizing colors; if patterned, add solid-colored cushions. Give old sofas new slipcovers to completely transform them. If your budget is limited, you might consider buying used furniture and adding slipcovers or refinishing it. Unfinished furniture is another option, although your choice of styles can be limited. It's also possible to buy furniture-making kits. (For more information on buying and refinishing furniture, see Chapter 14, "Furniture and Furnishings.")

You might be able to add some built-in furniture—such as a window seat or fitted shelves—to your living room. This takes up less space than individual pieces of furniture and also adds storage space.

ENTERTAINMENT

The living room is often used for entertainment of various kinds. Dinner parties and cocktail parties often take place at least partly in the living room, as do

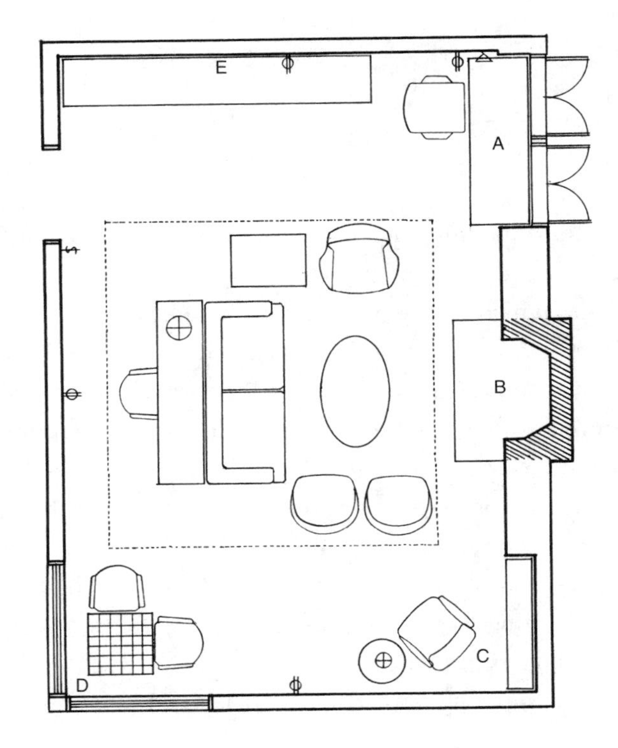

Living Room

A. *A window with a view is a good place for a desk. It can be used for letter writing or as a place for projects.*

B. *A fireplace is a perfect spot for a conversational grouping.*

C. *A quiet corner provides a place to read or play an instrument.*

D. *A corner window is a fine place for a game table.*

E. *A long, blank wall is the place to put shelves for books, stereo, CD player, tape deck, videocassette recorder, or TV. The TV can be placed on a swivel base to face various positions in the room.*

family and holiday celebrations. For such events you will often serve refreshments. A cocktail cart or tea cart can take the place of a wet bar or bar cabinet in a small room. In a pinch you could use a large, decorative tray to hold refreshment necessities. Of course, with the trend away from drinking alcohol, you will not need to store the variety of bottles, shakers, glasses, and stirrers once required, but you will no doubt still want to keep on hand a supply of coasters and napkins and possibly an ice bucket. Make sure your storage plans include room for these items.

Electronic equipment such as stereo components, a television, and a videocassette recorder can also be part of a successful party or gathering. Media or entertainment centers are collections of cabinets and shelves that can be configured to suit your equipment, lifestyle, and budget. Shelves should hold entertainment units at waist height or eye level for convenient operation. Use drawers and shelves below for storage of audiotapes, CDs, and videocassettes. Make sure the cabinets have the necessary openings for adequate ventilation and wiring.

LIGHTING

Pay close attention to lighting your living room. Many different activities go on there, all of which need to be properly lit. Most living rooms are fitted with a single central light, which hardly provides all the light needed. In general, there are three types of lighting: background, task, and decorative or accent. Living rooms often benefit from use of all three types. Background light can come from overhead fixtures (downlights or track lights), wall fixtures or sconces, or uplights concealed by furniture or plants. Lighting the walls (rather than depending on a single central ceiling fixture) makes a room seem larger. Task lighting for reading, sewing, and other activities can come from table lamps, floor lamps, or angled wall lamps. Desk lamps can be used to provide task lighting for writing tables or desks. Decorative lighting—of collections, artwork, wall hangings, and the like—can come from spotlights hung from a ceiling-mounted track system or recessed into the ceiling. (For more lighting ideas, see Chapter 16.)

STORAGE AND DISPLAY

The living room may have to accommodate a wide variety of useful and decorative objects, so storage is very important. Proper living room storage is also important for families with children, especially if your living room incorporates your dining room and playroom as well. Wall storage systems can supply bookshelves, cabinets, and space for electronic equipment. Separate storage pieces, such as breakfronts, armoires, secretaries, and chests of drawers, are a more traditional approach to the problem. A large round table used as a corner or end table can be very handy if you have the space for it. Draped with a floor-length cloth, the top can be used to show off books, vases of flowers, and collections of decorative objects, while piles of magazines, needlework, games, and other clutter can be stashed beneath, concealed by the fabric.

In small rooms glass shelves appear to take up less space. Depending on the thickness of the glass, they can hold small or large objects, although not heavy items such as a row of books. Consult with a glazier to determine the required thickness of glass to carry a specified weight over a given length. Mirrors also help to enlarge a space visually. Built-in window seats with lift-up lids or cabinet space beneath are a good place to store things that you want to keep out of sight.

A wall of storage units, whether custom-built or assembled from ready-made units, is obviously one place to start. The advantage of using these storage units, available from a number of sources, is their versatility in terms of configuration, price, and style. You might also find a large storage piece, perfect for your needs, in a secondhand or thrift shop or at a flea market. Another option is to employ baskets, wicker chests, or other offbeat containers to hold everything.

The living room is a perfect place to have lots of bookshelves. The spines of books provide an attractive background, and the shelf space can also be used for displaying pictures, accessories, and collections of objects. You can purchase unpainted wooden bookshelves and cabinets in various sizes and create your own units; buy finished wall units in wood, laminate, or lacquer; or even hire a carpenter to build custom ones. Bookshelves can be fitted with drawers or pull-out shelves to hold files, TVs, VCRs, stereos, sewing notions, or hobby equipment. Be sure to give careful consideration to the depths required for all of the items you intend to store on the shelves. Plan too for expansion.

Details, such as lamp bases, artwork, and decorative objects, make a room special and give it personality, distinguishing it from a well-put-together hotel room. Aim for a pleasing, lived-in look rather than cold perfection. When you are decorating or redecorating, it may seem that you have a lot of space to fill up—blank walls, tabletops, shelves—and very little to fill them with except clutter. Or you may feel you have too many things you want to display and have no idea how to show them off to their best advantage.

One place to display such items is on the wall. Collections of china and ceramics look good displayed this way; so do vintage dresses or even handbags and scarves. Also, you can frame anything that's fairly flat, such as a treasured antique textile or piece of embroidery; postcards or other varieties of paper ephemera, such as sheet music covers or autographs; and even small rugs or samples of vintage patchwork.

Tabletop or shelf arrangements can be created in the same spirit of experiment and improvisation, although you need to observe a few rules. One is that small objects should always be displayed in groups. Taller items should go in the back. Odd numbers are easier to arrange in a pleasingly casual way than even numbers. The smaller the object, the better it looks when presented in a group with other small things. Very small pieces, such as a collection of seashells, pretty polished stones, or old buttons or beads, can be poured into decorative glass jars, vases, or boxes for display. Another way to show off small objects is to group them according to color or material. If arranged with style, even the humblest collection can add charm and interest to a room.

FIREPLACES

A wood-burning fireplace makes a wonderful, traditional focal point for a living room. Beyond the warmth and beauty of a fire, a fireplace provides many decorating opportunities. The wall area above the fireplace is a traditional space to display decorative objects and art. The mantel is also an excellent place to show off a collection of objects, such as vases in china or silver, pottery figurines, or photographs of family or friends in attractive frames. Clocks, candles, and folk art are appropriate for manteltop display as well. Functional items such as fireplace tools and andirons can also be considered decorative accessories. You should select them according to the style and color scheme of the living room. For example, classic brass accessories look best in a formal room, wrought iron in a country-style room, and sleek chrome in a contemporary room.

EXERCISES

Use the questions and suggestions below to help you develop a new decorating scheme for your living room.

1. What is the function of the living room in your home? Is it a place for adults only, is it for adults and children together, or is it a special occasion room? Do you have a family room or does the living room do double duty? Are pets allowed in? If not, what is your strategy for keeping them out?

2. Do you prefer a formal or informal living room?

3. Does your living space focus outward (onto a view or outdoor space) or inward (on a fireplace or other focal point, such as a piano, an art display, or an entertainment center)?

4. What activities take place in the living room? List them in order of importance to you. (For example, entertaining, formal and/or informal; club or business meetings; playing of piano or other instruments; listening to recorded music; reading; watching television; studying; playing with children; board or card games.)

____

____

____

____

____

____

5. What will need to be stored in the living room? (For example, stereo equipment, records, tapes, CDs; cameras, photographs, slide projector, screen; television; toys and games, desk; books and shelves; piano or other musical instruments; art or collectibles display; firewood; bar supplies.) List items and where they need to go.

____

____

____

____

____

____

____

6. List each piece of furniture you now have in the room and note how it serves the activities and functions listed in questions 4 and 5. You should then have a list that will help you decide what new pieces you need or what you can get rid of.

7. Is there a place to put special holiday decorations, such as a Christmas tree or a menorah? Can you create such a place?

8. What alterations or adaptations (new painting or slipcovers, for example) will you need to make for the new decorating scheme?

5

THE DINING ROOM

Dining rooms, in theory at least, are relatively simple to decorate. You need a table and chairs, an overhead light fixture, a sideboard to store cutlery, china, and linens, and that's it. Few people, however, have the luxury of using a dining room just for eating meals. For most the dining room or area needs to be available for other functions. It might have to double as a workroom for hobbies or as a study for homework. Or you may not have a separate dining room at all; it may be an area in another room, such as a family room or living room. Kitchen-dining rooms are a familiar phenomenon; living-dining rooms are another common combination. In the case of the latter, it's often a good idea to define the separate areas visually with a change in materials, such as carpeting to bare floor, or with a physical division, such as a screen, a bookshelf, or a room divider.

Since food is served in this room, finishes should be as practical as possible: flooring should not show crumbs and should be easy to clean, sideboards or buffets should have pads to protect their surfaces from hot pans or baking dishes, and tablecloths and napkins should be washable. The table itself should wipe clean. Laminate tables with a high-gloss finish resembling lacquer can be very elegant; they come clean with the swipe of a sponge and are resistant to heat and nicks. Protect a wood surface with coats of furniture wax or polyurethane. Carpets and upholstery should be treated to be soil resistant. Your goal is to create a special occasion atmosphere within a practical, everyday framework. A dining room should be comfortable and functional, a relaxed place to enjoy your meal. Refer back to Chapters 1 through 3 to evaluate the space, decide on a color scheme, and think about what style you want to use in your dining room. Once you've created a decorating plan for the room based on the suggestions given there, use this chapter to answer questions and solve design problems peculiar to dining rooms.

TABLES AND CHAIRS

Dining tables come in many sizes and shapes; square, round, rectangular, and oval are the most common. You can figure out how big a table you need based on the number of place settings it needs to accommodate. A place setting is

CHECKLIST

1. Do you have adequate room to store all of your tableware, silverware, and linens?
2. Is the light over the table on a dimmer switch?
3. Have you measured the room and made a floor plan?
4. Do you have room for extra seating?
5. Do you have a sideboard for service?
6. Have you created a color scheme?
7. Do you need to add special details for entertaining?
8. Will the dining room be used for purposes other than eating? If so, have you made provision for those other activities, in terms of lighting, storage, and so forth?

approximately twenty-seven inches wide by fourteen inches deep; this includes room not just for dining implements but for diners' elbows as well (add two inches to the width if your dining chairs have arms). A rectangular table that will seat four comfortably should be about fifty-four by thirty inches; to seat eight, eighty-four by thirty. To seat four people, a round table should be thirty-nine inches in diameter; to seat six, fifty-two inches in diameter; to seat eight, seventy-two inches in diameter. A good table height for dining is twenty-eight to thirty-two inches; most dining tables are thirty inches high.

Chairs should have a seat height about ten inches less than the table height, so that they will fit comfortably under the table. Each chair needs approximately three feet of space behind it (in order for one to pull it out and then sit down). There must also be enough room for another person to pass behind the chairs. A minimum passageway is twenty-four inches, and a seated person takes up about twenty inches (with the chair pulled into the table), so allow at least forty-four inches between table and wall if you want to be able to walk comfortably around the table with a serving tray.

Expandable tables, with leaves, drop leaves, or pull-out surfaces, are useful. Two smaller tables that can be pushed together also provide more dining space for special occasions or large gatherings. Evaluate your dining table carefully. Remember that when a drop leaf is down, you won't be able to seat someone on that side of the table. Where are the legs on the table? Try to arrange place settings so that one diner doesn't end up straddling a leg. Also, if you are considering table and chairs that don't come as a set, make sure they will work well together; check to see if the chair arms fit under the table apron. (See Chapter 14 for more information on types of tables and chairs that can be used for dining.)

Extra chairs, such as folding or stackable pieces that can be kept in a closet or storage area, come in handy for festive occasions and large family gatherings. Built-in banquettes or window seats are another option—the table can be lined up with them to provide additional seating.

STORAGE

A serving trolley, sideboard, or buffet is a useful place to set down serving dishes, a bottle of wine, an ice bucket, or extra glasses. If your dining area is

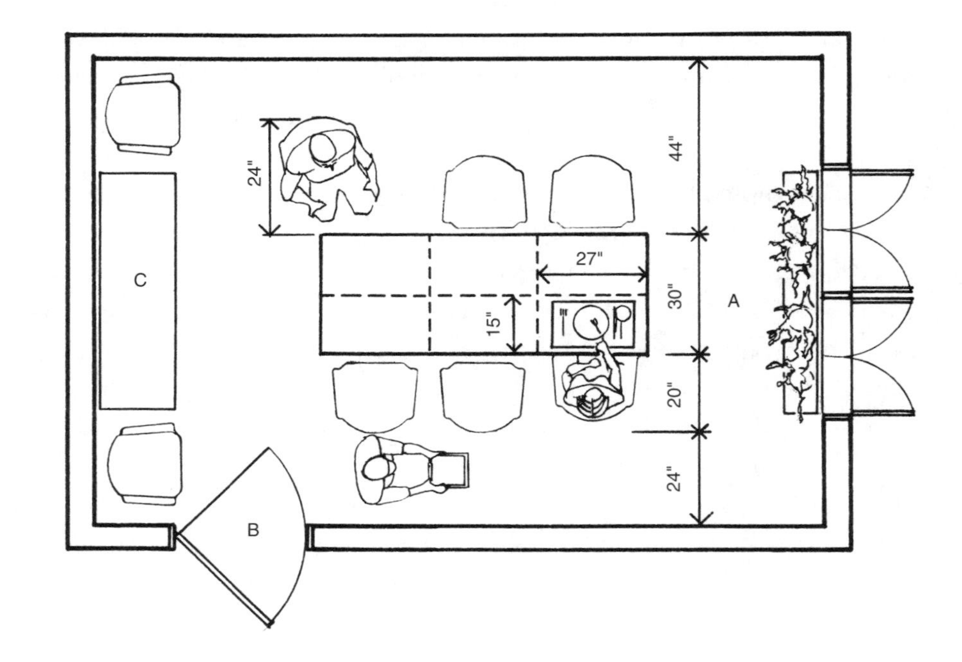

Dining Room Clearance

A. *Placing the long axis of a table perpendicular to a window allows the maximum number of people at the table to have a window view.*

B. *A door between a kitchen and dining room should swing in two directions.*

C. *For convenience a sideboard should be near the kitchen door.*

small, you may find that a wheeled cart is the best solution; it doesn't take up much space and can be stored elsewhere if necessary.

You will also need enough storage for all of the glassware and china not stored in the kitchen. The dining room is often a useful place to keep large serving pieces, silver flatware and cutlery, and fancy china patterns used only on formal occasions. A traditional china cabinet, buffet, or hutch is very handy. Drawer space can hold table linens, serving pieces, and extra silverware as well as such adjuncts of gracious living as candlesticks, vases, and napkin rings. A sideboard can do double duty as a bar for large parties.

LIGHTING

Proper lighting includes a fixture over the table. This light should be on a dimmer switch. Chandeliers or other pendant lights are appropriate; you might also want to install track lighting for more flexibility. Wall sconces or corner uplights can supply additional ambient lighting; a spotlight can add drama, whether it is trained on the sideboard to show off the food or focused on a special centerpiece for formal dinners. Bright light is not a prerequisite for the dining table. The overall desire is to create a mood, not to light up every nook and cranny, so lighting in the dining room can be dramatic and decorative rather than task-oriented.

If your dining table does double duty as a study table, a flexible lighting scheme is crucial. While your central over-the-table light can still be dramatic and decorative, you might want to make sure that with a dimmer it can be turned up to provide sufficient light for writing out math problems or checking tax information. An alternative is to keep small, inexpensive study lamps (the kind that fold up) in a drawer in the sideboard, or to angle track lighting to cast pools of light on the table. (See Chapter 16 for more information on lighting.)

DOUBLE-DUTY DINING AREAS

When dining areas are part of other rooms, the same rules of space, materials, and lighting apply, but the two spaces should also blend harmoniously and comfortably. In order to make such spaces work, you need to define the dining area carefully. Visually separate it, perhaps with a change in flooring, a low barrier, a set of bookshelves, a sideboard or buffet table, or even a low railing or a change in level—a step up or down. A curtain or folding screen could also be used as a space divider. Use different lighting or an area rug to give the dining area more definition.

Lighting changes can be as simple as low-key ambient lighting in the larger area combined with a spotlight on the table to center attention there when the light is on. Or you can add a decorative fixture that is turned on for dinner parties, in combination with candles on the table and the sideboard. A flexible lighting scheme will allow you to achieve a number of different effects (see Chapter 16 for more information).

You can also use a change in wall covering, paint effects, or window treatment (perhaps a tailored shade in fabric matching a favorite upholstered piece in place of full curtains) to subtly differentiate the dining area from the rest of the space. Remember, though, that you want to maintain the flow of the whole space, so try to keep some continuity through use of the same or similar colors and finishes, or the shared area will look arbitrary or chopped up.

Furniture pieces that are useful in the double-duty dining room include tables that can be put together to make one large surface or used separately. Tables with leaves are the traditional solution to lack of space. Built-in storage and work areas can double as dining surfaces in a small room.

EXERCISES

Use the following list of questions to help in planning a new scheme for your dining room.

1. How many people will eat in your dining room, both on a regular basis and on special occasions? Do you have formal dinner parties or do you prefer a more informal style of entertaining?

2. How much storage space do you need for china, cutlery, linens, table leaves, glassware, and other items (for hobbies and such)? Make an inventory of your tabletop possessions. Do you have enough space to store them now? How much more space will you need?

3. Do you use your dining room mainly at night or at other times of the day?

4. If it is used for activities other than dining, what are they? Do you have the proper lighting for these activities?

5. Do you think your lifestyle and needs will change in the near future—that is, do you plan to have children, or will grown children be leaving soon?

6. Do you plan to do more or less entertaining in the future? Will your table need to accommodate larger or smaller parties on a regular basis?

6

THE KITCHEN

Kitchens can be sleek workrooms or food pit stops or cozy family-gathering rooms. It seems as though there are a myriad of options for kitchen style these days, from retro to country to superfuturistic. Kitchens are like laboratories or workrooms, in that each one is as idiosyncratic as the person who uses it.

The kitchen is more than the sum of its parts. Kitchens aren't always what they seem—although state-of-the-art kitchens are in great demand, so is take-out food. Even if it is seldom used for cooking, the kitchen is often the center of the home, and people certainly do not want to give it up.

The kitchen is an interesting room to decorate. According to most surveys, it is one of the most frequently renovated rooms in the home. But redecorating is not just about tearing down walls and replacing appliances. Details count, especially if you're living in a rented apartment and you can't make structural changes. You can make a big difference with carefully chosen accessories, such as canisters, tea towels, spice racks, plants, posters, prints, and good-looking pots and pans.

The kitchen is one part of the house where you and those you live with will spend a lot of time. While you may not want to do major renovations, you still want to get the best you can from what you have. Before you begin to redecorate the kitchen, keep a notebook on hand in the room. Jot down work patterns, annoying problems, brilliant ideas, and a wish list—straight from experience. Apply this specific information to the planning techniques discussed in Chapters 1 through 3, then use the exercises and suggestions discussed below specifically for the kitchen, and you'll be well on your way.

CABINETS, COUNTERTOPS, AND STORAGE

Just as upholstered furnishings can determine the style of a living room, cabinets dominate the look of a kitchen. You may feel you are stuck with yours, either because you rent or because your budget won't permit you to replace them. But there are a number of small changes that will give your kitchen a new look without renovation. Of course, style may not be the only problem; the cabinets may be too small or inefficiently designed to hold all of your supplies and utensils.

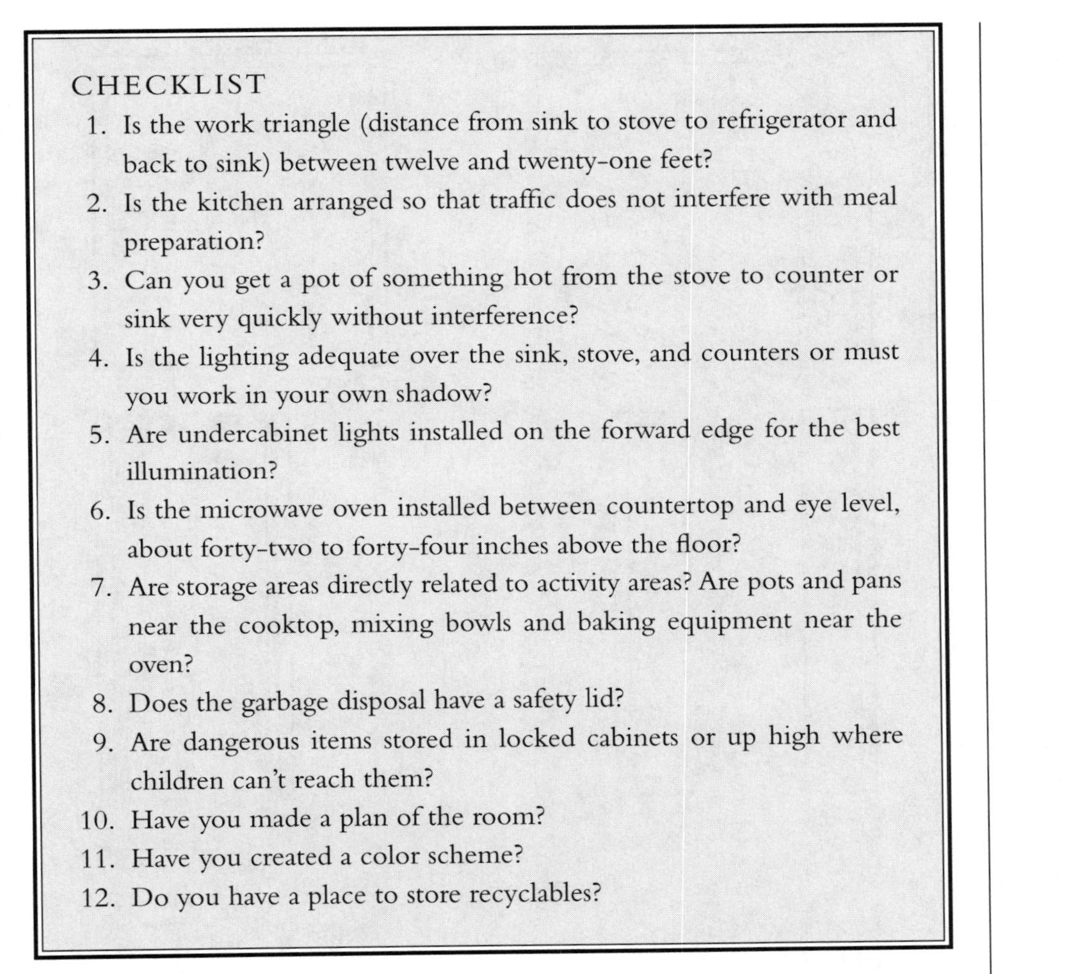

CHECKLIST

1. Is the work triangle (distance from sink to stove to refrigerator and back to sink) between twelve and twenty-one feet?
2. Is the kitchen arranged so that traffic does not interfere with meal preparation?
3. Can you get a pot of something hot from the stove to counter or sink very quickly without interference?
4. Is the lighting adequate over the sink, stove, and counters or must you work in your own shadow?
5. Are undercabinet lights installed on the forward edge for the best illumination?
6. Is the microwave oven installed between countertop and eye level, about forty-two to forty-four inches above the floor?
7. Are storage areas directly related to activity areas? Are pots and pans near the cooktop, mixing bowls and baking equipment near the oven?
8. Does the garbage disposal have a safety lid?
9. Are dangerous items stored in locked cabinets or up high where children can't reach them?
10. Have you made a plan of the room?
11. Have you created a color scheme?
12. Do you have a place to store recyclables?

Basically your options include repainting, resurfacing, or replacing the cabinets, or installing additional cabinets and retrofitting your existing ones with new storage devices, such as sliding trays, cup hooks, and lazy Susans. Repainting or refinishing cabinets is probably easiest. This is possible even for laminate surfaces if you use the right type of paint. If you don't want to repaint completely, you can add a stencil motif. Refinishing wood cabinets is similar to refinishing any piece of furniture. You can replace cabinet doors for a whole

Kitchen Plans

Movement of the kitchen work triangle—refrigerator, sink, stove.

L-SHAPED

- *Normally the dishwasher is adjacent to the sink. In this kitchen configuration, the work area in front of the sink would be blocked by the dishwasher tray, so the dishwasher is moved to the right.*
- *A shelf over the sink is a nice place for plants.*

U-SHAPED

- *Kitchen lighting should be balanced (without shadows). This can be accomplished by placing downlights on either side of work areas. Task lighting should be located over the sink and stove as well.*
- *The wall oven is located near the stove, with space for hot pans between.*

PULLMAN

- *The most used surface in a kitchen is between the refrigerator and the sink.*

GALLEY

- *A 2 ½"- to three-inch-wide shelf along the wall serves as a place for spices, towels, or cooking implements.*

(continued)

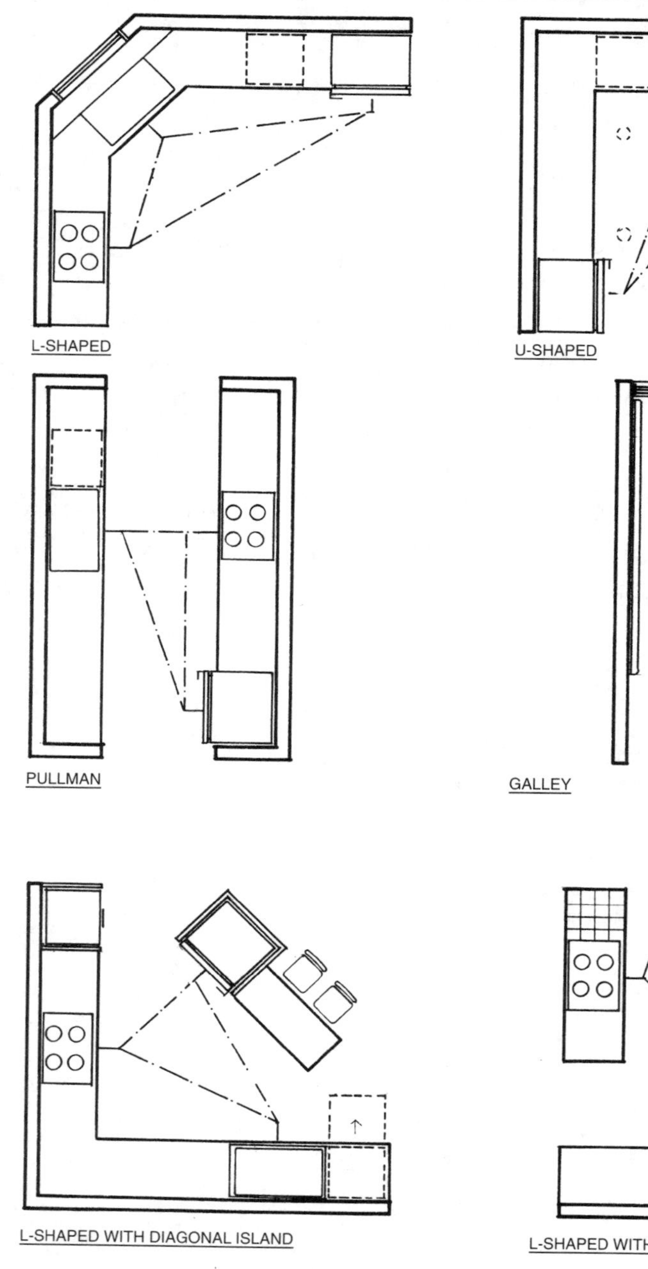

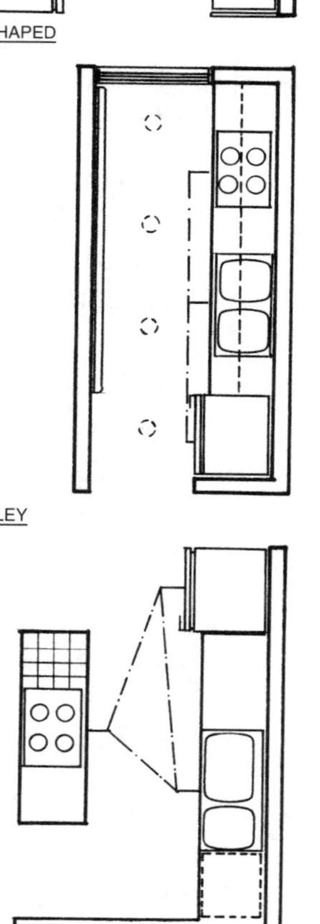

new look or leave them off entirely. You can also change the hardware on drawers and cabinets for a quick, inexpensive face-lift.

If you need more storage, try adding open display shelves. If you don't like looking at labels, you can store items inside canisters or baskets (which will also help protect them against insects). You can also install two- to four-inch-deep shelves for spices in the space between the countertop and wall cabinets, on the inside of cabinet doors, and on the end wall of a group of cabinets. These shelves can also be used to store cooking utensils, potholders, or dish towels—anything small that can be placed neatly out of the way to keep the work surface clear.

Organize your storage and work areas according to the way you work. Sort the things in your cabinets, putting little-used items out of the way so that there's more room for the things you use every day. Extra storage can be added by installing cup hooks on the undersides of cabinets, by hanging utensils on a wall grid, and by placing slide-out wire baskets below shelves.

All kinds of nifty, space-adding shelving can be found at a housewares store or through catalogs specializing in household items. (See pages 259–261 for the names and phone numbers of some of the most popular outlets.) These outlets feature adjustable sliding shelves and drawers and special racks for difficult-to-store items like pot lids. Another option is to hang a pot rack—several handsome models are available, in various metal finishes and sizes. Some double as shelves for cookbooks or houseplants. Some are hung from the ceiling, others from the wall.

Another relatively easy way to refurbish your kitchen without completely renovating it is to replace the countertops. You can also re-cover an existing counter with tile (you will need to consult a how-to book for complete details on the process; see the Bibliography for suggested reading). If your counter has square edges, it can be re-covered with laminate (round- or waterfall-edge counters must be replaced completely).

THE WORK TRIANGLE

In an ideal kitchen, the sink, stove, and refrigerator are an equal distance apart. This is known as the work triangle. If the work triangle is of proper proportions, you don't have to walk for miles every time you need to get something

L-SHAPED WITH DIAGONAL ISLAND

- *This unusual configuration increases the work area in front of equipment, which is highly desirable when two people are cooking together.*
- *The counter doubles as a desk or breakfast bar.*

L-SHAPED WITH PARALLEL ISLAND

- *A tile surface adjacent to the cooktop is the perfect place for hot pots.*
- *An island cooktop that requires a hood cuts site lines across a kitchen.*

from the refrigerator or awkwardly balance heavy soup kettles as you carry them from the counter to the stove while preparing a meal.

Here are the recommended dimensions: Each side of the work triangle should be from four to seven feet long. There should be a two-foot minimum of work space on either side of the sink. The dishwasher should be near (or preferably next to) the sink. Make sure there is enough room to open the dishwasher without adversely affecting circulation in the kitchen. There should be at least eighteen inches of prep space near the refrigerator and at least eighteen inches of space on either side of the stove. If you are replacing your cabinets, you should use these dimensions in your planning.

If you are not replacing your cabinets or if you can't make permanent alterations, you won't be able to change your work triangle. But you can make the work triangle more convenient by adding a work trolley or a tall table. If you can't add a new counter, try adding a cart with a butcher-block top. Be sure it is countertop height (thirty-six inches); many are not.

APPLIANCES

Appliances are important not only to how a kitchen looks but to how it functions. In the course of your redecoration, you may find it necessary to replace an old appliance, buy a new one, or find a way to make the old ones fit into the new scheme.

When replacing a stove or range, the first consideration is whether to get gas or electric. Which do you have? Should you change? Look for the bright yellow energy guide labels for energy-use comparisons. Gas-powered stoves are the usual choice of professional chefs. With gas you can tell by looking at the height and color of the flame how much heat is being produced, and it's easier to control the temperature. However, a gas stove can be harder to clean than one with electric burners, although sealed burners solve this problem, and there is also a small danger of carbon monoxide poisoning or leaks if your hookup is not properly sealed or the kitchen is not adequately ventilated. Of course, in many areas you can't get a gas hookup, and most apartment dwellers have no choice about type of stove. Fortunately, electricity has many advantages of its own.

Electric cooktops, the type installed in a counter without an accompanying oven, are the least expensive. Standard electric hobs (burners) have some disadvantages: they are slow to heat up and tend to retain heat, so cooking can go on even after you have turned the burner off. But electric elements are very reliable, clean, and safe. Halogen elements are more expensive because they combine the quickness and responsiveness of gas with the safety and reliability of electric burners. Glass ceramic cooktops, also more expensive than the regular enameled steel, are energy efficient, durable, and easy to clean.

Magnetic induction coils are the most expensive form of electric-powered hob. Electromagnetic energy is transferred directly to cookware (which must be made of iron or steel) through a glass cooking surface. There is heat only for as long as the cookware remains in contact with the surface; once you lift the pan up, the heat stops. Another safety advantage is that the surface will not burn you if you touch it, and there are no open flames or hot coils.

You may prefer a range, that is, a cooktop and oven built into one unit. A range can cost 10 to 20 percent less than installing a cooktop and a separate built-in oven. It is safer to buy a model with the burner controls at the front rather than at the back, where you may have to reach over a hot surface or open flame to use them.

Conventional ovens (as opposed to microwave or convection ovens), whether gas or electric, are the least expensive. They heat up the kitchen when in use but are great for baking. Convection ovens, available as separate units and with some high-end ranges, use fans to circulate the heat. They are more energy efficient than conventional ovens and keep the kitchen cooler, as they do not produce as much ambient heat.

In order to control grease and smoke, install a ventilation hood in your cooking area. You don't have to vent to the outside; many models have internal filters to trap grease and particles. Of course, these filters have to be changed on a regular basis.

Microwave ovens use high-frequency electromagnetic waves, which make the molecules of food move more quickly, creating heat that rapidly cooks the food. Microwave ovens are best for warming up liquids and leftovers, defrosting frozen foods, and cooking vegetables. They are a boon for dieters, too, since very little fat is needed for most food preparations. They are a poor choice for roasting or baking, because meat will not brown and bread will not rise properly. Microwaves also require special cookware. The best place to put a microwave is next to a heat-proof surface, so that food taken out can be set down without delay.

Refrigerators come in different shapes and sizes, but the technology is all the same. The main things you need to consider when replacing a refrigerator are size, efficiency, and which way the door should open. Most models have hinges that can be reversed. You can also buy a special twenty-four-inch-deep refrigerator that will fit flush with the front of adjacent cabinets (refrigerators are normally twenty-eight to thirty-six inches deep). A combination refrigerator and freezer can be one of four types: single door, side by side, freezer on top, or freezer on the bottom. The last one is considered the most efficient. Single-door styles are the least efficient, since the freezer unit has to work harder every time you open the door to take something out of the refrigerator. Side-by-side units are usually the most deluxe. The other option, if you have the space, is a separate refrigerator and freezer.

In a dishwasher the features to look for are capacity, quietness, ease of use, and energy-efficient no-heat or low-heat drying cycles. Other options that are useful include liquid rinse dispensers if you have especially hard water, food pulverizers, to grind up food residue, delicate cycles to protect fancy china, programmable start times, and automatic temperature monitors.

A variety of countertop appliances, from bread bakers to pasta makers, flooded the market in the 1980s. You must decide for yourself which of these items will enhance your cooking methods. These are in addition to such standard items as coffee makers, blenders, electric mixers, and electric can openers. Remember that small appliances in plain sight tend to clutter the countertops and those that are stored away tend not to be used. Some manufacturers have attempted to solve this problem with appliances that mount underneath wall cabinets or on the wall.

Most small appliances now come in a choice of white or black, so it's relatively easy to match finishes. Some high-end major appliances are available with front panels and trim kits that can be styled to match kitchen cabinets for a custom, built-in look. If you have an older but still functional appliance from the era when wood tone, copper, and avocado were the preferred colors, you

flour
sugar

can change the color with automotive paint. In some areas there are painting services that will refinish appliances to fit a new color scheme.

LIGHTING AND WIRING

Is your kitchen lighting adequate? You need task lighting over work areas as well as general lighting from a ceiling fixture. To get more light on your work surfaces, install fixtures beneath wall cabinets and over the sink and stove. Make sure under-cabinet lights are installed on the forward edge for the best illumination. Ceiling lights should be placed with care; they should not be put so far away from the counter that you end up working in your own shadow. Track lighting is a convenient way to augment ceiling-mounted fixtures; it has the advantage of flexibility, since the individual fixtures can be moved to cast light where needed. However, open-track systems can be annoyingly efficient attractors of dust and grease. Closed-track systems, while less flexible, are easier to keep clean. To establish a comfortable lighting level in your kitchen, be sure to consider the overall square footage of the room and the height of the ceiling.

If you can't install recessed downlights or track lighting, try clamp-on work lights or surface-mounted fluorescent fixtures. Add a pendant light or ceiling fixture over the eating area if there's not one there already. The pendant bulb should be out of your line of sight when you're seated. Either type of fixture should have a dimmer switch. An accent light, such as a wall- or ceiling-mounted spotlight, can be used to show off decorative accessories.

In order to ensure a better lighting scheme for an older kitchen, you may have to call in an electrician to install additional wiring. While you're at it, make sure you have an adequate number of outlets. The suggested placement of electrical outlets includes a duplex outlet—which accepts two plugs—every four feet, a duplex outlet on an island workstation, and a fourplex near a serving counter. A plug strip along one countertop wall is useful if you like to keep all of your small appliances in the same spot. There are special electrical requirements for stoves, wall ovens, and exhaust hoods, as well as special safety requirements for outlets near sinks, so be sure to consult a licensed electrician before installing new wiring or appliances.

FLOORING

Another relatively simple way to change the look of your kitchen is to change the floor. New tiles or resilient vinyl flooring, for example, can give it a very different look. Tile possibilities range from rustic quarry tile to brick to ceramic, expensive but elegant marble terrazzo, and even wood. Resilient vinyl flooring, the old reliable, comes in sheets or tiles and is available in a number of colorful, decorative patterns, as well as rather convincing imitations of all of the above natural materials, at a fraction of their prices. If you are changing the type of flooring in your kitchen, check the subfloor to make sure it can accommodate the new load. Floors of all types (with the exception of ceramic tile) can be painted, although the color choices are limited. Apply polyurethane to a painted floor to protect it against wear. Because much of your time in the kitchen is spent standing, the resiliency of the floor should be considered in terms of the stress it imposes on your legs.

EATING AREA

Kitchen eating areas are usually small and informal, intended for intimate family meals or casual occasions such as breakfasts and snacks. You might have a built-in eating area with banquette-style seating or a small table and chairs. A fold-down table that attaches to the wall is a good alternative for a small kitchen. It can be installed thirty-six inches above the floor for use as a snack counter or at the normal table height of thirty inches. You can choose your seating to match your eating area—folding chairs for truly tight space or backless stools that can do double duty at work counters, allowing you to rest your feet while peeling vegetables or cutting up a chicken for frying.

RECYCLING

New laws and concern for the environment mean that recycling now affects almost everyone. The big question for many people is where to put recycled items before they go to the recycling center or get picked up. If you are lucky enough to have a deep drawer that you can spare, designate that as the recycling drawer. Line it with ordinary paper bags or use plastic bags from the supermarket. Good dimensions for a recycling drawer are twenty-four inches deep by thirteen inches wide by twenty inches high. You can also buy a variety of ready-made bins for holding cans and glasses, or use a second wastebasket for recycling and a box for newspapers. A good houseware or hardware store should have a selection of such containers. Another possibility may be to use cabinets beneath an island or peninsula counter as a recycling storage area.

DECORATIVE ACCESSORIES

Your kitchen, like every other room in your home, benefits from attention to decorative details. Although the kitchen is primarily a working area and must first of all be functional, little touches make a big difference. There are lots of fairly easy ways to give your kitchen a new look. Put up new wallcovering with a scrubbable vinyl surface for easy care. Change the windows from café curtains to venetian blinds in an accent color; add a decorative valance; put glass shelves across a window to display plants or pretty bottles; repaint the woodwork around the windows to pick up a color in the new window treatment.

Grow plants, anything from culinary herbs to scented geraniums. The kitchen is often warmer and more humid than the rest of the house, so it's a good place for growing things. Hang potted plants from the ceiling or put them in windows.

Try treating the walls in a new way. Retile or resurface the backsplash (the wall area between the counter and wall-hung cabinets) for a change of pace. If you don't want to wallpaper or repaint, add paneling or floor-to-ceiling shelving to provide additional storage as well as a country kitchen atmosphere. You can use the shelves to store sundries in canisters or to organize your cookbook collection properly. Add a bulletin board for a cheerful effect and to keep family schedules current.

EXERCISES

Redoing a kitchen is often as much a question of reorganization as it is redecoration. It will help you to make proper redecorating decisions if you first evaluate how you use your kitchen. The following questions are designed to help you get started.

1. Will your situation change in the near future (will more or fewer people be using the kitchen)?

2. What kind of cooking do you do—simple, elaborate, or some of each?

3. How often do you shop for groceries, how much do you buy, and, consequently, how much storage space do you need?

4. Do you have enough counter space or do you have to keep moving things around to clear space for chopping, mixing, and other tasks?

5. Can you find things easily in your kitchen, or are all of your storage spaces crammed full?

6. How do you prefer to store your spices, on a rack or in a cabinet? Do you separate them into cooking and baking spices?

7. Do you like the look of open shelving or open storage, or do you find it too messy?

8. Where do you keep cleaning equipment and supplies? Do you have a convenient place for them?

9. Do you need or have a place to store wine?

10. Are dish and flatware storage areas close to the dishwasher? Are storage areas directly related to activity areas? Are pots and pans by the cooktop, mixing bowls and baking equipment by the oven, and so forth?

11. Make a list of all kitchen items, including furniture, utensils, spices, and such, that you need to accommodate. To set priorities, divide the list into three sections: basics, options, and luxuries. Do you have enough storage space for small pieces, cutlery, serving pieces, food items, pots and pans, table linens?

12. Does your kitchen have enough electrical outlets? Do you have any special requirements for the placement of electrical outlets? If you want to add electric appliances, is there a place to plug them in? Is the outlet adequately rated for the equipment?

13. Even if you don't plan to update your appliances during redecoration, it's a good idea to make an appliance chart for future reference. List the appliances you have, when they were purchased, and their make, model number (if available), electrical rating, color, and size. This way, when you do need to make a new purchase or replace an appliance, you'll have the information you need at hand.

14. Keep in mind that the kitchen, while the cheerful center of the home, can be a very dangerous place, especially for small children. Make sure your kitchen is safe. Does the garbage disposal have a safety lid? Are dangerous items stored up high or in locked cabinets?

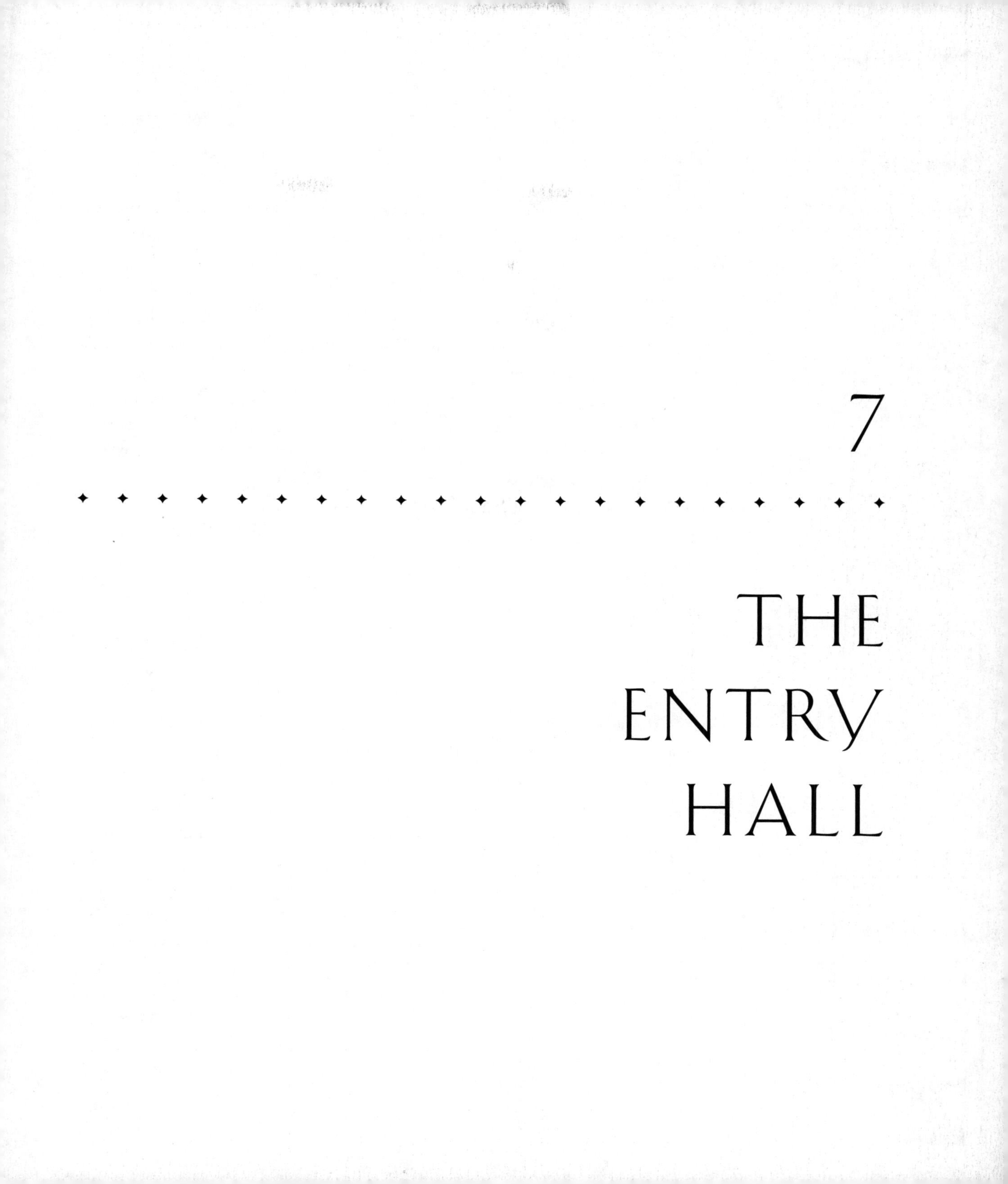

7

THE ENTRY HALL

As the first introduction to your home for guests and the last space you pass through before you leave, the entry hall plays a small but important role. It will immediately reflect your taste and will give visitors a sense of the rest of your home. Your main desire in decorating it is to make it warm and welcoming.

In general, the entry hall has to coordinate with the living room, since the two are usually only steps apart, as well as with other areas of the house and the stairs in a two-story home. But decorating this space is not just a question of style; although an entry hall might not get a lot of use, the use it does receive is significant. Refer back to Chapters 1, 2, and 3 to make sure you've covered all the bases in terms of your color scheme and chosen style. The decorative style of the entry should, of course, harmonize with the rest of your home, but since this is a small space, it's your chance to go all out, with expensive materials and dramatic effects. The ideas given here can also be applied to other entrance areas in your home, such as the passage from the garage to the kitchen.

STORAGE

Lots of things end up in entry halls, from scarves to extra sets of keys to road maps and old address books, if only because there's no place else to put them. It's a good idea to have a fairly large table or even a chest of drawers or desk here. Another possibility is a piece of furniture like an apothecary chest, with drawers that will hold mittens, scarves, rain hats, and small umbrellas. If your entry hall is too small for a piece of furniture of this size, try to fit in a narrow bench, a small table with a drawer for keys and sunglasses, or even a wall-hung shelf with a drawer beneath and a stool. If you don't have the ideal—a hall closet—then at least have a free-standing coat rack or a wall-mounted row of hooks to hold coats, both for your own household and for guests. If you have a telephone in this area, you will need space for directories as well as a place to sit down.

CHECKLIST

1. Can a caller be seen through a window or peephole without opening the door?
2. Does the entry have a hard-surface, easy-to-clean floor (ceramic tile, stone, terrazzo, well-varnished hardwood)?
3. Is there a guest coat closet nearby or a place to store coats, such as a coat tree?
4. Is there a coat closet for family members near the most commonly used entrance?
5. Is there a place to sit down and put on or take off rain and snow boots and other gear?
6. Is there a spot to stash a wet umbrella?
7. Is there a convenient place to put keys and the mail, a handbag, briefcase, or knapsack?

TABLES

You will need a place to set things temporarily in this most transient area of your home. The top of a storage piece, such as a chest or shelf, will do, or you might want to add a small table for keys, mail, and packages—things that you want to make sure you take with you or need to put down while you put on or take off your outdoor gear. Tables also serve as a surface for displaying small items, such as an arrangement of fresh or dried flowers, a small drawing or painting on an easel, or a collection of pottery figures.

MIRRORS

Large mirrors are useful in hallways, not just for checking your appearance but also for creating the illusion of more light and space. The best place to put them is over a table, chest, or shelf, or anywhere that makes the entry seem more spacious.

In addition to mirrors, entry halls are generally a good place to display things on walls—photographs, drawings, embroidery, sketches, or any small framed object. Since this is usually a small space, it's a particularly good place to put items that might look lost on a large wall.

SEATING

Historically, the proper chair for an entry hall was known as a hall chair, a rigid, upright wooden seat that provided a place for servants and tradespeople to wait in grand country houses. It was traditionally unpadded and uncomfortable. Although it's unlikely that you'll be receiving visits from tradespeople or petitioners, the entry hall is a place where you might need to sit and wait for a moment or put on or remove snow boots and other outdoor gear. You don't have to go against tradition with an overstuffed upholstered armchair; a bench or a backless stool will do.

LIGHTING

Lighting is important in hallways for safety's sake—to let residents of the house see who wants to enter, to help newcomers see where they're going—as well as to create a welcoming first impression to your home. The exterior of the front door should be well lit for the same reasons. You also need to have sufficient light to use a telephone or mirror if these items are in the area.

The best fixture choices for an entry hall are recessed downlights and wall- or ceiling-mounted fixtures aimed at the wall (see Chapter 16 for more information on these types of lighting). They take up little space, do not collect dust, and go with any style of furnishings. A less expensive alternative is track lighting, which is flexible. Track lights can be surface mounted and powered from a single outlet. If all you have is a single ceiling light, use a powerful bulb and add a dimmer switch, or consider replacing it with a decorative hanging fixture. You can supplement any of these arrangements with a table lamp and uplights in the corners.

FLOORING

When you are choosing flooring for the entrance hall, durability should be the first consideration. Since people coming in from outside bring dust, dirt, and damp in with them, this is not the place for fragile antique rugs. Door mats, although utilitarian, don't have to be unattractive and are very useful here. The best practice is to have two, one outside the door and one inside.

The choice of durable materials is quite extensive. Ceramic tile, marble, quarry tile, terrazzo, brick, flagstone, and slate, while in general somewhat expensive, may be affordable here since the floor area is relatively small. Wooden floorboards do well if sealed with a hard-wearing polyurethane finish, although if you live in the country, where you bring abrasive materials such as dirt and gravel directly into your home, you may want to use more durable flooring. Even vinyl flooring can look good as a less expensive alternative, and it will certainly take the wear. Carpeting is generally not a good choice because ground-in dirt weakens the fibers, and traffic causes wear and tear. Carpeting is also more difficult to clean.

Small area rugs can be used to brighten up a hallway. They can be moved aside in bad weather and often can be washed in the washing machine, making them easy to maintain. Just be sure to put them atop nonskid mats or secure them to the floor with carpet tape in order to avert accidents.

EXERCISES

Although the entry hall is a small room in most homes, it plays an important role in your decorating scheme as the first room seen by visitors. The questions below should help you in planning the decoration of your entry hall.

1. Is there a visual separation between the entry and the living room? Do you feel you need to create one?

2. Does the flooring need to be replaced? What type of flooring do you prefer? Calculate the floor area of your entry by multiplying the length times the width to get the square footage. With this information you can determine the cost of replacing the flooring.

3. Is there enough space to keep everything you need in your entry? Is there a place to put coats?

4. Make a list of changes you'd like to make in your entry hall and how to put them into practice. For example:

    a. Change flooring—install terrazzo tile. Buy area rug.
    b. Repaint walls and repaper dado. Choose paper and coordinate paint color.

____

____

____

____

____

____

____

____

____

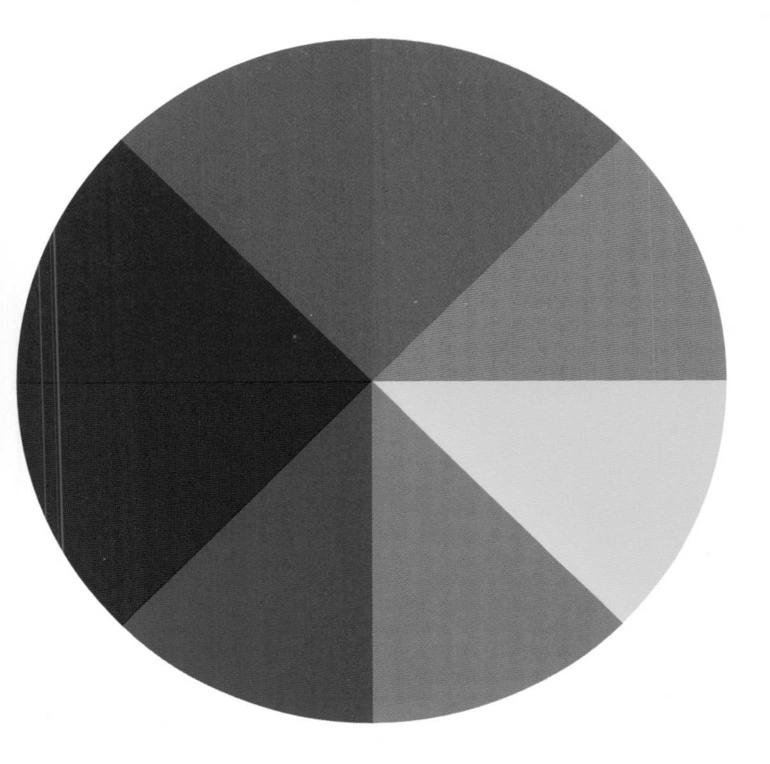

The color wheel shows relationships among colors. It can be used to develop color schemes. Related color schemes, also known as analogous colors, usually combine three neighboring colors on the color wheel. Complementary color schemes use two colors opposite each other on the color wheel. Triadic schemes are based on three colors equally spaced around the color wheel.

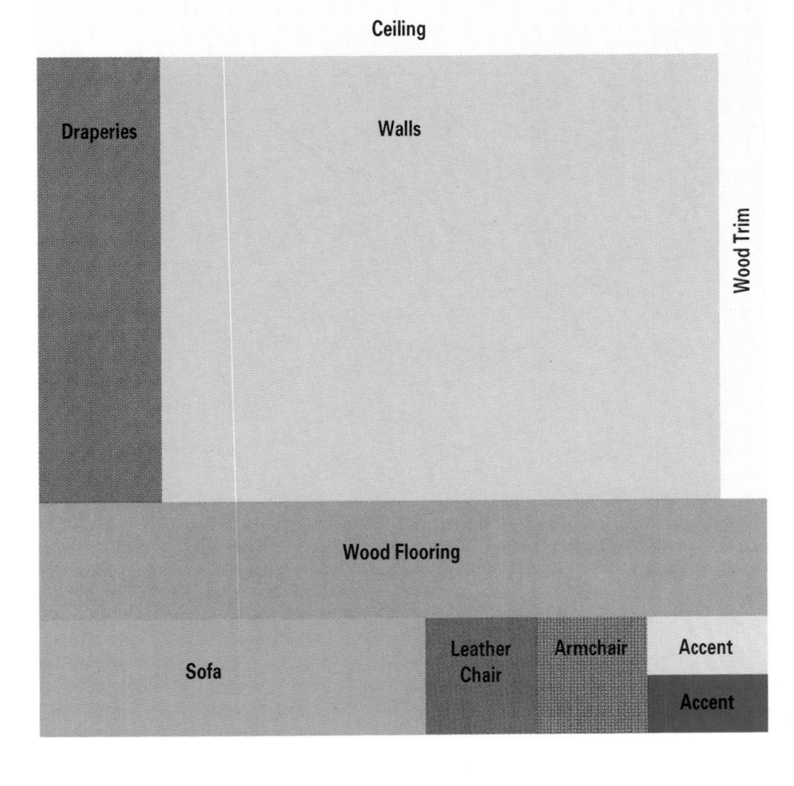

A quick glance at a color chart will let you know if your room scheme combines colors in harmonious proportions. Here is a color scheme for the living room shown two pages following. The pale lavender tint on the walls echoes the deeper lavender on the window treatments. Both are complemented by the warm coral color of the sofa. Off-white, taupe, and cool green keep the sophisticated scheme in balance.

GEWERBE
MUSEUM BASEL
NEUES
WANDER
AUSSTELLUNG
DES DEUTSCHEN
WERKBUNDES
12. FEBRUAR BIS
11. MÄRZ 1928
10-12h & 14-19h
BAUEN
GEOFFNET 10-12, 14-10 UHR

ABOVE: *Custom-built bookcases demonstrate how book-lined walls can be a strong decorative element. Drawings and a collection of folk art are also displayed on the shelves, while simple, overscaled furniture is covered in an unusual combination of pastels. The uncommon color scheme gives the room much of its style. (Copyright © John Hall)*

TOP, LEFT: *Gracious but not stuffy, this living room takes the edge off its grandeur with casual, wrinkled slipcovers and woolen plaid throws on the upholstered furniture. A collection of flea market finds and whimsical reproductions adds flair. (Copyright © John Hall)*

LEFT: *A carefully assembled collection of Marcel Breuer–designed furniture is complemented by a coir rug, a pony-print ottoman, and contemporary posters. Chrome, glass, and black leather are the hallmark of the early-twentieth-century Bauhaus style. (Copyright © John Hall)*

ABOVE: *A sleek, modern kitchen glows nevertheless from the warm wood tones used in the cabinets and flooring. Pinpoint spotlights and touches of chrome add drama, while mulberry miniblinds add a bit of analogous color. (Courtesy IKEA)*

LEFT: *A traditional kitchen uses color in unexpected ways. The countertop is blue tile, which provides a pleasing contrast to the reddish-brown quarry tile used on the floor. White, employed extensively on walls, cabinets, and trim, keeps everything cool. (Copyright © John Hall)*

ABOVE: *A stylish but small dining area gains impact through the clever use of color combined with neutral tones. The soft gray-and-white floor and white walls provide a perfect backdrop for multicolored glassware and a combination of modern and traditional art, furniture, and lighting. (Copyright © John Hall)*

RIGHT: *A warm, traditional dining room mingles walls painted a deep terra-cotta color with painted and stained wood and the graphic punch of bright white and black. The kilim underfoot brings it all together. (Copyright © John Hall)*

Graphic, overscaled blue-and-white gingham checks dominate this bedroom, giving it an updated country look. Various details reinforce the overall scheme, such as the tab-topped curtains at window and bed tied onto pale pine pegs, a mirror in a rustic frame, and the white-and-brass bed frame. (Copyright © John Hall)

Southwestern style and brilliant colors define this rugged but comfortable bedroom. A scattering of rugs underfoot adds comfort, while the pale yellow ottoman at the foot of the bed is a sophisticated grace note. (Courtesy IKEA)

5. As the gateway between your home and the rest of the world, the entry hall is a place to think about safety and security. Can a caller be seen without opening the door (through a window or peephole)?

6. Is lighting adequate to identify callers and for visitors to see where they are going?

7. Make a list of security considerations and how they might affect the decoration of your entry hall.

____

____

____

____

____

____

____

____

____

____

8

THE FAMILY ROOM

A family room can be a lot of things—a playroom, a dining room, a second living room, or maybe all of these things combined. This is a room where lots of different activities may take place, from the quiet (reading, sewing) to the electronic (watching television or videos, listening to music, playing computer games) to noisy group enterprises (games such as pool or table tennis). It may be a big room or a small one.

One thing to remember about decorating a family room is that comfort is the first concern. Of course, you want the room to look good, but since this is a place to kick back and relax, indulge in hobbies, or just sit and talk, it is important that comfort and ease take precedence over formality and contrived decorative effects. The style of your family room as well as its substance should convey informality and good times. Coziness comes from deep, soft, comfy seating, warm colors, sensible materials, and lots of pillows and cushions for lounging. Color combinations are relaxed rather than uptight and overly matched. This is a room to have fun in, so it doesn't have to be impeccably coordinated.

Use the procedures and suggestions given in Chapters 1 through 3 to get started. These techniques will help you evaluate what you like and don't like

CHECKLIST

1. Do you have sufficient storage space for hobby equipment and leisure-time pursuits?
2. Is there adequate task lighting?
3. Are the materials—flooring, wallcovering, upholstery—good-looking, hard-wearing, and easy to care for?
4. Have you created a color scheme?
5. Have you measured the room and drawn an accurate plan?
6. Have you decided what furniture you need to buy?
7. Have you thought about reusing existing furniture?

about your present family room, decide which changes to make, set your priorities, and make your final plans about new furniture, a new color scheme, and any other changes you want to make. Use this chapter to discover the specifics of decorating a family room.

FURNISHINGS

The family room is a place for relaxing and having fun. The furniture should be comfortable and sturdy. This is not the place for delicate antiques, it is the place for big, solid sofas and handsome upholstered chairs; even the sometimes unattractive BarcaLounger or La-Z-Boy chair has a place in the family room.

Perhaps the best way to arrange furniture is according to activity groups: a conversational group, perhaps, with a separate reading area and a play area. These don't need to be strictly defined. The play area might be near a spot where toys can be stashed; the reading area needs a light and a place to put a book; in the conversation area people need to be able to sit close enough to hear each other talk without distractions. Two sofas placed back to back might be a good way to divide up space—one side for conversations, listening to music with headphones, and other quiet activities, the other for play. The success of such arrangements will depend on the size and shape of your room.

Family rooms tend to be tucked away from the other rooms in the house. In older homes they are often situated in a renovated basement or attic and, as a result, may be subject to climatic extremes or damp.

In any case, flooring, upholstery, and other materials should be rugged and washable. Vinyl flooring, washable rugs, indoor-outdoor carpeting, washable wall coverings or paint, and paneled walls are all suitable for use in a family room, as are easy-care upholstery fabrics and slipcovers. Laminate surfaces make good sense for built-in furniture and case goods because they wear well and are easy to clean.

Closely patterned fabrics with small prints show dirt less readily than do solids or large prints. Wood or vinyl floors are easier to clean than light-colored carpeting, but solid-color vinyl can show scratches and dirt. With new soil-resistant finishes, wall-to-wall carpeting is also a viable option, and rugs can be taken up and cleaned as needed.

LIGHTING

Family rooms benefit from the use of general and task lighting. Display and accent lighting are at a minimum here, since this is a highly informal room. Floor lamps can provide either general or ambient light. Translucent fabric shades diffuse light best for general ambience, followed by linen, cardboard, and paper. Wall lights may be used as well. They are best if they are used directionally, to bounce light off the ceiling or floor. Directional lamps, reading lamps, or work lights should be adjustable to shed light where it is needed.

Track lights can provide a lot of light from a single outlet. They are very useful if you need to install additional lighting and can't afford to have a lot of expensive electrical work done. The track mounts to the ceiling or wall and can be fitted with floods and spots to provide lighting where needed. In terms of style, they are best suited for use in a casual or modern room.

Flexible desk lights or floor lamps with flexible necks are great for use in the family room, since they can be pointed wherever they are needed. It's also good to have lamps that are on a dimmer switch or will provide various levels of light, since some activities, such as watching television or using a computer, require different illumination than do reading, playing the piano, or sewing.

STORAGE

Built-in storage is especially useful in a family room. Cabinets and bookshelves provide ideal places to stash away board games, hobby equipment, videotapes, and cameras. If a hobby area or home office is part of the family room, closed storage is a special boon, since evidence of interrupted projects or works in progress can be shut neatly behind closed doors when it's time to use the room for something else.

Depending on what you use the room for, you might need space for such items as drawing boards, yarn, art materials, or a sewing basket. In addition you will want to provide built-in work surfaces or perhaps a large worktable. Large baskets or a wooden chest make unusual storage containers.

Wall storage systems that incorporate shelves, cabinets, and space for electronic equipment are well suited for the family room. A wall of storage units, custom-built or assembled from ready-made units, can provide all the storage you need. They can incorporate entertainment equipment—television, VCR, and stereo system—a drop-lid desk, open shelves for books and decorative objects, and cabinets to hold hobby supplies and conceal junk. Wall systems are available in a variety of styles, finishes, and price ranges. You can purchase unpainted wooden shelves and cabinets in various sizes and create your own units, buy a ready-made system from one of the large houseware outlets, or hire a cabinetmaker to build a system that fits your exact space and needs.

ENTERTAINMENT CENTER

The entertainment or media center, which incorporates electronic equipment such as televisions, stereo equipment, video games, and VCRs, has become the new high-tech hearth. Entertainment is on call for the family at the click of a remote control. The family room is an appropriate site for this equipment, and an entertainment center, a collection of shelves and cabinetry designed specifically for the purpose, is an ideal place to house it all.

Entertainment centers are smaller than wall systems and can be either wall hung or freestanding. They are specifically designed to hold electronic equipment and accessories, including audiotapes, videocassettes, and CDs. They can be combined with a larger wall system or used in conjunction with other types of storage.

You can choose between open or closed storage. A closed unit has doors that either swing out or retract; when closed the unit simply looks like a wall of cabinetry. Closed shelving reduces dust buildup considerably. Glass doors for stereo cabinets are especially useful. If they are made of smoked glass, they conceal the unit somewhat while still allowing the remote to function without opening the doors.

Open shelving reveals the equipment, putting it on display and making it the focal point of a room. Both closed and open storage have their advantages. Some people prefer closed storage for electronic equipment because it keeps the room looking neater; others like being able to see everything at a glance on open shelves. If you do opt for a closed unit, you may find that sliding or retracting doors are the best bet; a hinged door takes up space when opened, which can be inconvenient in a small room.

Practically speaking, the best entertainment centers hold the equipment at waist to eye level for convenience, with storage for tapes and CDs below. When purchasing a unit, make sure that the design conceals all of the cables and wires and provides adequate space for cables to lead out of the cabinet to power outlets. Remember to check that the unit is deep enough to accommodate your equipment. Some televisions, especially older models, are deeper than the standard eighteen inches. You should also make sure that units have enough ventilation to release the considerable heat generated by some electronic equipment.

CHILDREN'S ACTIVITIES

If your family room will play host to many children's activities, look for surfaces that will wear well, will take a lot of abuse, and are nontoxic and not likely to cause injury to a child. Imaginative graphics on walls, floor coverings, and fabric will help your children learn while playing.

Think of the playroom as a living room for your child. Try to establish an open area for your child to play in. Along the outer edge of the space, you can supply play equipment, anything from a rubber mat to a box of toys. You will probably want to set up a child-size worktable for drawing, painting, and playing with clay. You might also want to provide a quiet area with pillows, a floor rug, or even a hammock. How many of these items you want to incorporate into your family room and how many you think should be located in the child's bedroom is, of course, up to you. Plan ahead for flexibility. Your child will pass through many stages before leaving home.

GUEST ROOM

With the addition of a sofa bed, the family room can become the guest room. But it takes more than a bed to make a guest comfortable. Anyone who is staying longer than overnight will need a small area to store personal belongings, perhaps a drawer or at least a basket or a portion of a shelf. Another thoughtful thing to provide is a coat tree or closet space (if you have it to spare) where clothes can be hung up. Even a wall hook will do. A place to put small items of clothing, such as belts or shoes (perhaps a belt hanger or a concealed shoe bag hung on the back of a door), is another helpful touch. A final luxury for any guest is a good reading lamp, along with space next to the bed for personal items such as wristwatches and eyeglasses.

With the current emphasis on a casual lifestyle, the family room has become the center of activity for many contemporary families. A well-decorated and properly set up room, with sufficient storage and hard-wearing materials, is a real asset. Too often the family room, like the bedroom, is last on the list when it comes to redecorating, since it's often only seen by family members and other "insiders." If you have a formal living room, the family room might be a place to let your more colorful, casual side come through. If your kids use the family room often, get them involved in creating the new decorating scheme. If the whole family participates, then it will become a room that the whole family wants to use.

EXERCISES

The family room plays many roles. Use the questions below to help you plan your new decorative scheme. You might also consult other chapters in this section, particularly Chapter 4, "The Living Room," and Chapter 5, "The Dining Room."

1. Is the family room currently a place where you like to spend a lot of time? Is it busy in the morning and evening only or is it used during the day as well?

2. Is the family room a single-purpose or multipurpose room? Is it a place where a group of people will all do one thing or where several people will pursue individual hobbies?

3. Make a list of activities that take place in the family room. Are there any you'd like to add? Next to each activity, list which equipment and supplies are required.

___

___

___

___

___

___

___

___

___

___

___

4. Sketch out a plan of how you intend to store or otherwise accommodate equipment and supplies.

5. If the family room will sometimes accommodate overnight guests, is there appropriate storage, lighting, and privacy for them?

9

THE HOME OFFICE

The home office presents a unique problem in decorating. Too often it's an afterthought, since most homes weren't designed as workplaces. One of the first problems in decorating the home office may be figuring out where to put it. If you have a separate room, that's great, but what if you don't? Creating an efficient working space in a multipurpose room takes careful planning.

Even if you don't work at home full or part time, you can benefit from having a space for paperwork, whether it's doing your taxes, paying the bills, writing letters, or organizing charity work. And if in addition to all these activities you bring papers home from the office occasionally, you've probably found yourself wishing for a better place to work than the dining table.

To help you plan your office, use the guidelines given in the first two chapters for making an overall plan and choosing a color scheme. Although in most cases your home office won't be seen by anyone but you, your family, and close friends, it should still be a cheerful, well-organized area, a place where you can concentrate and get things accomplished.

CHOOSING A SPACE

The good and the bad aspects of working at home are two sides of the same coin: lack of commute versus lack of physical and psychological distance from your work. Some people like to work in their bedrooms; others need to be as far from the bed as they can get. If you're at home alone during the day, you'll probably have more choices about where to locate the office than if you are looking for a space to use in the evenings and on weekends.

In either case, an area outside the routine course of household activities works best for a home office. If you don't have a door you can close, perhaps you can locate the office space in an area that's partially screened off from other home activities. Some spaces to consider are a spare or guest bedroom; renovated areas in garages, attics, and basements; a former dressing room or pantry; or even a large walk-in closet—any space that can be transformed from its present use into an area that's at least psychologically, if not physically, separate from the rest of the house or apartment.

CHECKLIST

1. Have you decided where you want your office to be?
2. Have you measured the room and made a floor plan?
3. Is the wiring adequate for all of your office equipment?
4. Is there proper task lighting?
5. Do you have enough storage space?
6. Have you created a color scheme?
7. Have you decided what furniture you need to buy?
8. Have you checked with an accountant to see if your home office is tax deductible?

If you live in an apartment or a small house, you may have to locate your office in a dual-purpose room. You can apply the same strategies for dual-use rooms as suggested in other chapters (see Chapters 5, 8, and 10), including using bookcases, an armoire, or other furniture to create a partition or arranging a screen of paper, fabric, or wood to conceal the work area.

Since the formal dining room is seldom in constant use, it may be the ideal choice for your double-duty room. A table, for example, can be used as both a worktable and a dining table. A desk can serve as a sideboard or a serving table. Also, bookshelves make a pleasant background for dining. Storage units with folding doors can be fully closed to provide a neutral background, and the doors take up less space when opened.

If you share a bedroom, it is probably not a good idea to allocate one end of the room as office space. If the bedroom is sufficiently large, however, so that an office area can be partitioned off in a way that allows one person to work while the other reads or sleeps, then this choice is perfectly viable. The same goes for partitioning off a part of the family room or living room.

One way to ensure at least acoustical privacy for the home office is to use sound-deadening materials in its decoration, such as wall-to-wall carpeting, acoustical ceiling tile, and cork-lined walls (which can serve as a bulletin board as well). Shelves filled with books also make natural sound blockers.

If you will be meeting with clients in your home, you'll need a separate meeting area, preferably one large enough to hold a table and chairs—about fifty square feet. Of course, your living room can double in a pinch, especially if at-home meetings with clients are rare.

COUNTERTOP, FILING, AND STORAGE NEEDS

Careful attention to storage for reference and working materials is a priority in planning the home office. When you're working without the support of an assistant, organizing your files is especially important. Filing cabinets are utilitarian but can be concealed. Ordinary metal ones can be painted to blend with the wall. More expensive ones of laminate or wood look decorative on their own. If you absolutely can't stand the way they look, they can be hidden behind a screen or in a closet.

You'll also need sufficient working surfaces as well as storage space. U-shaped and L-shaped work areas keep everything close at hand. A compact L-shaped working area takes up about five feet of space on one wall and six feet along another. One leg of the L could extend into the room as a peninsula if this arrangement is more convenient.

The simplest desk is a flush door on top of two filing cabinets, which are available in various heights. In addition to legal- or letter-width drawers for hanging file folders, you can find file cabinets with shallow drawers designed to hold pens and pencils, paper clips, floppy disks, personal phone books, notepads—all of the detritus of modern-day office life. Other specialized office furniture is discussed later in this chapter. If your work area is not large, consider keeping the items you use regularly in the work area and storing little-used items in another part of the house. For example, records that you need to keep for legal reasons but rarely consult can be stored in a filing cabinet in the garage or attic. Supplies bought in bulk can be stashed out of the way too. Remember to make sure that these "out of the way" supplies aren't "out of mind" as well—keep a list of where you've put what, and make sure that they are carefully packaged to avoid damage from mold or mildew.

Don't skimp on work and storage spaces—the rule of thumb (akin to Murphy's Law) is that you will always need more than you think you'll need. The amount of papers, records, and archives to store will always get larger, never smaller, no matter how diligent you are about throwing things out. Plan for more than you need. Since many storage units are modular (from vertical file cabinets to cases for bound volumes of professional journals), try to plan for adding at least one more than you need now.

Even if it seems as if you'll never use the extra space, office equipment needs change all the time. You may want to add a fax machine or a desktop copier or a new printer for your computer. You can always use the "extra" space to hold vertical files, boxes of supplies, or ongoing projects. If you have a large desktop work area, you can use the space beneath it for storage of seldom-used reference materials or office supplies. Overhead cabinets and wall-hung shelves are other good methods of getting work-related items out of the way and yet still having them close at hand.

In a dual-purpose room it's all the more important that work can be neatly stored away. If you have extra closet space in a joint bedroom and office or guest room and office, you can use that. If necessary, you'll also need to think about how to conceal equipment that's not in use, such as with screens or curtains. Some tried-and-true concealers include under-bed storage, roll-top or lift-top desks, and a table with a floor-length skirted cloth, which will effectively hide anything underneath.

FURNITURE

The overall style of your office is up to you. There are many types of office furniture available, from no-frills models with enameled tubular steel frames to solid wood executive-style furnishings with brass hardware. There are also special desks for computers, rolling carts designed to hold files, and desk chairs that range from molded particle board to down-filled leather. You can even decorate with antiques.

Since everyone's working style is different, it's best to stick with what you've found has worked well for you in the past. If you're short and have trouble sitting comfortably at a desk, you have several seating options: you can get a chair with adjustable height or a footrest, or you can buy a separate footrest. This will help you maintain correct posture. A tall person can choose a chair with a tall back and an adjustable seat. People with back problems may want to try a Scandinavian-style kneeling chair.

If you use a computer most of the time, a chair with arm rests (plus a separate wrist pad on the desk) will help prevent fatigue. A swivel chair on casters lets you move easily from one part of the office to another without having to get up. Printer carts and stands make it easy to manage paper and equipment. Printer stands can also be adapted to hold fax machines (which often have their own built-in stands) and small copiers .

If you use a drafting table, which is usually higher than a standard desk, you will need a stool with a footrest as well as desk space next to the drafting table to store equipment. Some chairs adjust from drafting table height to desk height, saving you the cost and space requirements of two types of seating. Art supply stores are good sources for much equipment, particularly modular storage on wheels. Many such units, designed to hold myriad art supplies in various slots and cubbies, can be adapted to hold regular office supplies conveniently and neatly. Often art supply and office supply companies have mail-order catalogs and will deliver to your home.

LIGHTING AND WIRING

Try to place your desk so that natural light enters over the opposite shoulder from your dominant hand (over the left shoulder if you are right-handed; over the right if you are left-handed). While natural light is great, positioning a computer screen in front of a window can cause problems with glare. If glare is a problem during certain times of the day, invest in blinds or shades to block the light.

Good lighting prevents eyestrain. You should have a task light at your workstation. This can range from a snazzy matte black Eurostyle adjustable desk lamp with a swing arm to a simple clip-on light from the hardware store. It should be adjustable so that you can focus it on different areas, depending on the task, and positioned so that it doesn't cast shadows on your work. If you work at a computer, very even light is best, rather than just a light on the screen. An overhead light can be fine in a small room if it doesn't create shadows.

Other basics include proper wiring for computers and other office equipment. You may want to add a separate electrical circuit, depending on how much electronic equipment you have. In order to enforce your sense of self-sufficiency and privacy, you may even want to install some luxury extras, such as a personal coffee maker, a small refrigerator, and a radio or tape deck. These may also require additional wiring.

If you use a personal computer, you'll need to get a surge protector (also called a surge suppressor) to protect your data against abrupt changes in current caused by lightning or brownouts. The simplest way to provide this kind of protection is to buy a unit that is plugged in at the outlet. If you're having an electrician put in another circuit, however, surge protection can be installed at the same time. A similar type of device for telephone lines—needed if you transmit files via modem—is called a spike protector.

If you use a modem or fax machine frequently, you will probably want to install a separate telephone line. Before doing so you will need to make a plan for the layout of your office, in order to install the new phone jacks in the most convenient places.

EXERCISES

1. Make a list of what you most need to store—for example, professional journals, reference books, binders (empty and filled), correspondence and bills, books, software and diskettes, stationery, office supplies, manuscript pages.

____

____

____

____

____

____

____

2. Make a second list of what types of storage are necessary to accommodate the items on your first list—for example, file cabinets, bookshelves, vertical files, flip files for diskettes. Think about where to put them and indicate on your floor plan where they will go (see Chapter 14 for more information on average sizes).

3. What equipment does your "dream office" have? For example, do you yearn for more drawer storage, a place to keep unanswered correspondence, space for a photocopier, better lighting, more shelf space, more file storage space, a coffee maker, a refrigerator, or a sound system?

4. Make a second list of ways to create your dream space—for example, buying new filing cabinets or an old-fashioned desk with plenty of drawer space, clearing out a closet and adding a new electrical circuit for a photocopier, buying new shelves, adding lighting.

____

____

____

____

____

____

5. Make a list of your electronic equipment (such as a personal computer and printer) and any that you plan to buy in the future (fax machine, copier, new printer). Also list any changes in wiring necessary to accommodate them; you may want to make these changes now. Make a plan of your future office, with new acquisitions marked, to see if you will need additional storage or countertop space.

____

____

____

____

____

____

10

THE BEDROOM

You spend a lot of time in the bedroom—at least according to the statistic that the average person spends a third of his or her life asleep. The bedroom is where you get started in the morning (a delicate process for many!) and end each day. In between you might take a nap, read a book, or just meditate there. It's a place where you keep many personal possessions, including clothing, jewelry, and books. There's no denying that this is one room of the house that plays a very important role in your life, and yet, because it's not a "public" room, it is often neglected when it comes to decorating.

Your bedroom, since it is a very personal space, should express your personal style, whether it's exotic or down-home, elaborate or simple. You might want to use patchwork quilts or sumptuous filmy silk draperies. You might want to go all out to create a fantasy bedroom with a tent-draped ceiling. On the other hand, you might prefer to keep things plain and uncomplicated.

Use the information and advice given in the first three chapters to get started making plans, choosing a color scheme, and determining the overall style of your bedroom. (For a discussion of decorating a child's bedroom, see

CHECKLIST

1. Have you measured the room and made a floor plan?
2. Have you chosen a color scheme?
3. Is there proper lighting for reading in bed, for putting on makeup, and for checking your appearance in front of a full-length mirror?
4. Do you have enough storage space?
5. Is the bed placed so that morning light will not shine directly into your eyes?
6. Have you decided what furniture you need to buy?
7. Does the window treatment block out light? Noise?
8. Have you allowed a minimum of fifteen inches of space on either side of the bed?

Chapter 12.) Then use the details given below to help you deal with the design issues specifically relating to bedrooms, and you'll be off to a good start in redecorating this personal room to suit your needs.

SERENITY, COMFORT, AND PRIVACY

The bedroom is a place where you are often in a vulnerable and relaxed state. It is also a place where you should feel comfortable and safe, where you should have everything the way you like it. It's not always possible to achieve perfection, but at least you can try to get close to it.

For many people, controlling the natural light coming into the room contributes to creating that feeling of comfort. If your bedroom faces east you will be awakened by the morning light. Some like this sensation; others would rather be tortured. Position your bed so that sunlight doesn't fall directly on it at any time of day. Blackout shades and lined curtains, drawn to block the light, will ensure that sun haters and light sleepers will remain undisturbed.

Noise can also be a problem in bedrooms. While you seldom can do much about eliminating outside noise from traffic, you can try to insulate your bedroom against such disturbances by using sound-deadening materials in your decorating scheme. Fabric, for example, absorbs sound; fabric-hung walls (you can add cotton batting underneath for even better acoustic protection) or a bed canopy (again, quilted hangings increase the effect) will help, as will a carpeted floor and multilayered window treatments and lined curtains. Bookshelves filled with books are also good sound absorbers.

Color and texture are also important in making the bedroom a cozy, serene place. See Chapter 2 for more on color and emotion. A bedroom that is serene and uncluttered is the most restful. Though it isn't always easy to maintain a tidy bedroom, it is well worth the effort to try. Following are some suggestions for getting rid of clutter.

Closet Planning

A. *Two-inch-deep shelves with raised edges, mounted on the inside of the door.*

B. *Shelves for hats, sports equipment, and storage.*

C. *Double-hung rods.*

D. *Pull-out wire baskets four, eight, and twelve inches deep.*

E. *Rod for long garments.*

F. *Shelves for shoes.*

G. *Mirror mounted inside the door.*

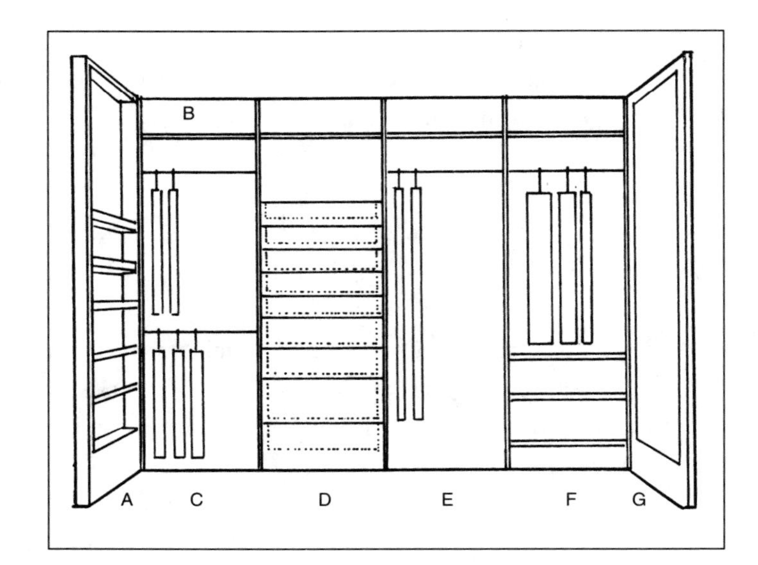

STORAGE

Most bedrooms have inadequate storage. By improving the storage in your bedroom, you can get the junk out of the room or at least get it out of sight, and make the room more serene. There should be twelve to eighteen square feet of closet space in a bedroom shared by two people and six to eight square feet of space in a bedroom for a single adult.

Built-in storage is the optimum solution, since you can use every inch of space. Built-ins offer many advantages over freestanding pieces. They use all the available spaces, from floor to ceiling, and give a neat, coherent look to the room.

If you don't want an entire built-in system, you might want a custom-fitted wardrobe. This handy piece of furniture can be built in or movable and can be custom designed to hold all of your possessions in a neat and efficient manner. Decide what you want to keep in it first and then order the wardrobe (not the other way around). The height of the wardrobe should be determined by how high you can reach comfortably (it can be somewhat higher if you're willing to use a stepstool). The depth of the shelves should depend on what will be stored.

Many people feel it's better to store folded items on a shelf rather than in a drawer because you can see everything on the shelf at a glance, whereas in a drawer you can see only the top layer of items.

If you don't want built-in storage, perhaps because you live in a rental house or apartment, you have several different options. Try to use as many double-duty pieces as possible. Platform beds can have storage drawers underneath for bed linens and other bulky items, and in some designs the headboard has cubbyholes or shelves that might hold anything from books to a small stereo system. Large baskets can provide neat, colorful storage that is also decorative.

Old standbys such as bureaus, chests of drawers, and blanket chests can serve to store many things, from sheets and towels to out-of-season clothing. With cushions on top, a blanket chest can serve as seating as well. Wall-hung shelving at the head of the bed and bookshelves at the foot give a custom, built-in look and are very useful for storage. Bedside tables should have drawers and shelving for extra storage. Many people like to watch television in their bedrooms but don't know where to put the set. You can conceal a television in an armoire (make sure the shelf is sturdy enough to hold the weight) or put it on top of a bureau or chest of drawers.

In order to make existing closets more efficient, there are several services, such as Closet King or California Closets, that will send a consultant to your home to help you figure out how to get the most use out of existing storage. The consultant can then supply you with all of the nifty space savers you need. These are franchise operations, so look in the phone book to find out if there is one in your area.

If you want to refit your closet yourself—adding extra shelves, double-height clothing rails, shoe racks, and handbag shelves—you can order the items you need from mail-order houseware catalogs. You can also find closet fittings and get shelving cut to size at your local housewares or hardware store.

FURNITURE ARRANGEMENT

By far the biggest concern in decorating a bedroom is where to put the bed. Some bedrooms are so small that fitting in a bed may seem impossible. To begin with, you'll need a minimum of fifteen inches on each side of the bed (for ease in making it). After that it's up to you. It will help to know standard American bed sizes, which are as follows:

Twin	39 inches (width) by 75 inches (length)
Extra-long twin	39 inches by 80–84 inches
Full or double	54 inches by 75–80 inches
Queen	60 inches by 80 inches
King	72 inches by 80–84 inches

These may vary slightly (there's nothing really standard about bed sizes).

Experiment with different arrangements on paper first, using your room plan, as detailed in Chapter 1 (moving a bed is often a major task). Placing a bed on the diagonal or in the middle of the room often produces a surprising feeling of spaciousness, depending on the size of the room. You might also try placing the head of your bed against a window—but maintain access to the window and be aware of the problems associated with dust, drafts, heat from a radiator, and possible outdoor sounds. The sill can serve as a headboard, providing storage space, and your curtains supply a decorative frame for the bed, thus unifying the room elements. If the room must accommodate two beds, you could put them head to toe or at right angles. A storage unit containing shelves or cabinet space could serve as a joint headboard.

If your bedroom is also a living room or home office, you might want a bed that is part of a wall unit (known as a Murphy bed). These units can include a concealed bed as well as nightstands, bookcases, lighting, and storage for clothing. Although it must be fastened to the wall when installed, it is not a permanent fixture, so if you rent your house or live in an apartment, you can take it with you when you move.

You can also divide up a large bedroom by using movable screens, well-placed shelves, or a built-in divider. One side of the room could be a sleeping area, the other could be used as a wardrobe or dressing area or home office (for more on home offices, see Chapter 9).

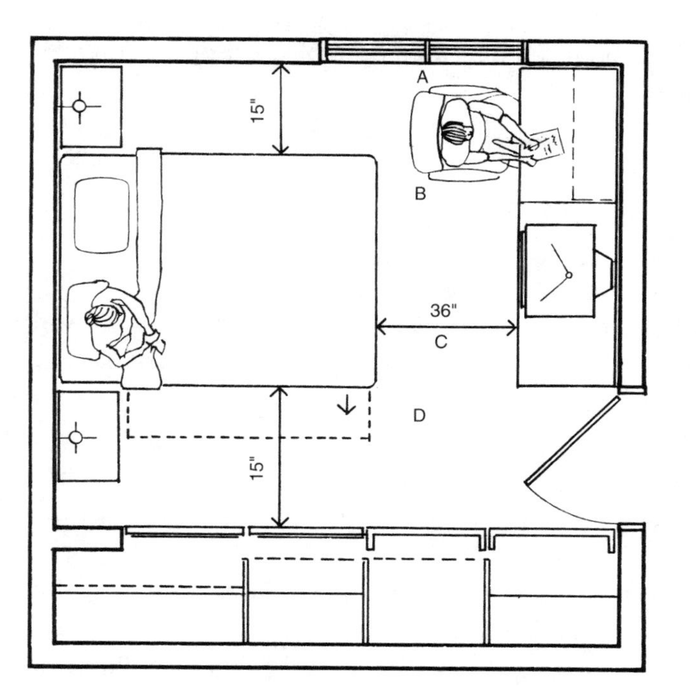

Bedroom Plan

A. *If you are an early riser or like to awaken to a room filled with sunlight, arrange your bedroom so that the head of your bed is oriented toward a window facing east.*

B. *A desk next to a window is a place to work, read, or put on makeup. Bookshelves can be mounted above the desk or bedside tables.*

C. *Clearances shown are minimum.*

D. *Storage drawers can be placed under a platform bed.*

LIGHTING

Lighting in a bedroom is more important than you might think. You need it for many activities—to wake up, to read, to apply makeup, to get dressed. One overhead fixture simply will not do. Among the fixtures you'll need is a good bedside reading lamp or one on each side of a double or larger-size bed. You can put the reading light on a wall, to free the bedside table or floor area. Wall-hung or table lamps with switches located on the cord are easiest to reach when lying in bed.

You also need good light by a full-length mirror, to check your attire. If your bedroom is large enough to be divided into different areas (a dressing area, a reading area), each will need its own task lighting, from lamps next to the chairs to lights over a makeup mirror.

Bedrooms should have controlled lighting. Put dimmers on all of the switches. This will ensure, in a shared bedroom, that one occupant isn't blinded by the other's reading light. You can also buy tiny reading lights that clamp to the pages of a book, to keep from disturbing your partner if you like to stay up late and read.

DECORATIVE ELEMENTS

You can add individuality and style to the bedroom in a variety of ways. It can be accomplished by adding something as simple as a custom-made bedspread or duvet cover or as elaborate as a full-scale canopy and bed hangings. You can add personality with plants, new curtains, and fabric pillow shams and cushions that coordinate or contrast with the rest of the furnishings. You might take a pretty little chair in cane or wicker and drape it with a flea market find—a patchwork quilt or a shawl. To add softness to the room, you can drape the bedside tables with fabric or lace.

Hang prints or posters that appeal to you. Add new tiebacks or a contrasting border to freshen up your curtains if you don't want to change them completely. To brighten up the walls, add a stenciled or wallpaper border, perhaps picking up colors and motifs from the bedspread or curtains.

Sheets and bed coverings are an important decorative aspect of a bedroom. Choose patterns and colors you like and find restful. Some people want to sleep only on plain white cotton, while others are more adventurous. You can be extravagant with sheets, on the whole, since they are widely available and can usually be purchased on sale or at a discount. A variety of duvet or comforter covers provides a quick change of looks.

Little touches are important. Make sure the waste basket is big enough and not constantly overflowing. Choose a bedside table that's big enough to hold everything you need, from a lamp, clock radio, box of tissues, and book to a carafe and water glass.

If your bedroom is small, there are techniques to enhance the existing space: Place mirrors at right angles to the window, for example, which has the added benefit of increasing light. Diagonal designs also seem to stretch space. Using a monotonal color scheme or repeating the same pattern or coordinated patterns for walls, upholstery, and curtains can help too. If you paint large pieces of furniture (the bedstead, bureau, or armoire) to blend in with the walls, they will seem to take up less space.

If you live in a rental house or apartment and can make only cosmetic changes to the bedroom, here are a few suggestions. If you have ugly carpeting or other flooring, put down your own rug—yes, even over existing wall-to-wall carpeting. This will immediately serve to make the room your own. Change the window treatment. Even if you're not allowed to take down existing window hardware or curtains, you can still make changes, such as putting new tiebacks on the existing curtains. If you can go further, put up your own ready-made curtains on the hardware already installed. If there are no blinds, find out if the landlord will let you install some. Plants are a good way to cheer up a bedroom quickly. Put small flowering plants on the windowsill or large plants in pots on the floor. Use them as screens to conceal ugly fixtures or wall coverings.

Finally, make the room your own with really eye-catching bed linens. This will make a big difference. You can also add coordinating accessories, from a bedskirt to a tablecloth and curtains. To create a focal point to distract from unsightly features, add coordinating bright cushions and cover unattractive walls with posters or large, colorful drapes of fabric or even a bright Chinese kite or Japanese kimono.

EXERCISES

1. Do you prefer your bedroom to be light and bright or dim and shadowy? Where does the light come from and how do you plan to control it?

2. Do you want to sleep in a cozy, confined area? Or would you rather have an open, airy space?

3. Do you read in bed? If you share a bedroom, will you need two reading lights (one per person)?

4. Ask yourself the following questions to determine how much storage space you need.

   - How much clothing will you need to store in your closet or wardrobe, both seasonal clothing and clothing that is out of season?
   - Will you be storing jewelry and hats as well?
   - How many sweaters do you own, and how much space do they take? Are there other folded articles for which you need shelf or drawer space?
   - How much space do your hanging garments take up? How long are the longest hanging items?
   - How many pairs of shoes do you own, and how do you prefer to store them (in the original boxes, in a hanging shoe bag, on shoe trees, and so on)?
   - What other things might you want in your custom wardrobe—a fold-down ironing board with a place to store the iron, a niche for shoe-cleaning supplies or a sewing box?
   - Do you have a linen closet or do you store bedding in your bedroom?

5. Do you want an area for sitting and relaxing in your bedroom? A study area with a desk? Where might you put them? What specific furniture would they require?

11

THE BATHROOM

Bathrooms can be hygienic closets or luxurious shrines. They can double as dressing rooms or home gyms. They combine decorative possibilities with many practical problems of storage and safety, humidity and heat. Often they are too small, only rarely too big. But you can take the problems inherent in decorating a bathroom and use them to your advantage.

Because it is small, the bathroom is a good place to use luxurious materials. You will need only small amounts of expensive materials and won't have to spend a great deal. Color, mood, and accessories are important in a small room, so changing the color scheme and the accessories will have a big impact.

The bathroom is the most renovated room in the American home, second only to the kitchen, although it may seem the least receptive to redecoration. The fixtures and fittings seem permanent, unmovable. You may feel as though you are stuck with a tile color you detest or a toilet and sink in a style you can't stand. While in some cases this may be true, you can do a lot to improve many aspects of your bathroom through careful planning and redecoration.

Make use of the suggestions given in Chapters 1 and 2 on making an

CHECKLIST

1. Is there an exhaust fan?
2. Do the tub and floor have slip-resistant finishes?
3. Have you supplied a place to hang a bathrobe and towel within arm's reach of the tub or shower?
4. Do you have enough towel rack space (two feet minimum) for each person who will be using the bathroom?
5. Is there a grab bar next to the tub or in the shower stall?
6. Is the lighting sufficient? (There should at minimum be a fixture above the mirror and one on either side at eye level).
7. Have you created a color scheme?
8. Will the bathroom be used for other purposes, such as a home gym? If so, have you made provision for those other activities?

overall plan and budget and choosing a color scheme. Then read this chapter for information that pertains specifically to the bathroom.

SAFETY

Safety is important in the bathroom. It's often a room full of sharp corners and hard surfaces that are slippery when wet. The bathroom can be dangerous particularly for the very young and the very old. But a practical approach can minimize many of the risks. First of all, both the tub and floor should have a slip-resistant finish. If your existing tub is slick porcelain, add stick-on nonskid strips or a rubber bath mat. See the section on flooring (page 150) for suggestions on nonskid floors.

For convenience, provide a place to hang a towel and bathrobe not more than twelve inches from the shower or bath. There should also be a grab bar within the tub enclosure and next to the tub. It should be at least three-quarters of an inch in diameter, easy to grasp, slip resistant, and capable of supporting a three-hundred-pound nonmoving load. Grab bars for a shower stall should be located just outside the entrance and within the stall, about forty inches from the floor. Wall-hung soap dishes should be at about the same height to prevent fumbling. In other words, you shouldn't have to bend over to get your shampoo, soap, or washcloth.

Lever door and faucet handles are easier to grasp than regular knobs. Low shelves make it easier for children old enough to bathe themselves to reach things that belong to them—bath toys, child-safe shampoo, towels. Young children also need a sturdy step stool in order to reach the sink.

LIGHTING

The combination of a ceiling fixture with a light on either side of the mirror at eye level gives the best lighting (it's easiest if all three are on the same switch so you can turn them on all together). Incandescent bulb lighting combined with full-spectrum fluorescent lighting, which is the closest to sunlight in color, is the best kind of artificial light for applying makeup. Diffused light is easier on the eyes than direct light, so make sure the bulb has some type of shade, whether a simple tube of frosted glass or plastic or a more elaborate style. If you like to read in the tub, you might want to add a reading light nearby. Just make sure that the light is securely mounted out of the range of the shower spray and under no circumstances can fall into a water-filled tub. A wall- or ceiling-mounted adjustable fixture is the best choice.

If your existing bathroom light is adequate but ugly, go ahead and change the fixture. Just make sure to maintain the same level of light. Also, there are special waterproof fixtures that can be added in the shower stall. Keep all cords and outlets away from water. If you are adding outlets, put them at shoulder height, which is generally safer and more convenient in the bathroom. This will help to keep small personal appliances, such as electric razors and blow-dryers, out of the danger zone.

FLOORING

Bathroom floors, above all, should be slip resistant and hygienic (sealed). This is especially important for children, who like to play in the bath and often get the floor wet. Examples of slip-resistant, waterproof flooring include specially treated cork, linoleum, studded rubber tiles, and slip-resistant ceramic tile. It should be noted that even when treated with a slip-resistant finish, ceramic tile is not the safest of materials—it's slippery even when slip resistant and hard, not resilient—so if safety is your primary concern, it should not be your top choice. Another consideration is that anything breakable dropped on a ceramic tile floor is sure to break.

You can use mats or rugs with a nonskid rubberized backing, place rugs on nonskid matting, or tack them to the floor with double-faced carpet tape. You can also lay down wall-to-wall acrylic carpeting, which is easy to cut out using a pair of heavy-duty scissors (but again, make sure it is fixed down around the edges to prevent wrinkling and rumpling). Acrylic carpeting is generally inexpensive, washable, and available in a wide range of colors, although it is not particularly durable. (See Chapter 18, "Floors," for more information on choosing and installing new flooring.)

FIXTURES AND FITTINGS

Depending on the type of sink or toilet fixture already installed in your bathroom, you may be able to replace it without too much trouble. The general rule is that you can replace an existing fixture with one of the same type or slightly larger if the piping remains in the same location. If the sink is a drop-in basin type, you can choose a new one in a different style or color but of the same shape or size and drop it into the existing cutout in the vanity top. You can also replace the entire vanity top, changing not only the style and color but the size and shape of the sink as well. If your existing sink is a pedestal sink, you can replace it with another one with a base the same size or larger (in order to conceal the mark on the floor left by the original sink) or with a wall-hung or drop-in sink in an enclosed vanity. The same rule holds for replacing toilets. Changing the type or style of a bathtub or shower is more complicated and will require the services of a plumbing contractor. Be aware that in a multiple dwelling, when you change roughings (piping), the entire space must conform to the new Americans with Disabilities Act.

Your fixtures can be resurfaced by painting with epoxy paint, although it's generally best to have this done by a professional. The technique is relatively simple, but it takes a lot of time, attention, and skill in the use of muriatic acid. You could also try a decorative paint technique such as sponging or stenciling on the outside of the tub or give it the European touch of a wooden enclosure.

While changes like these will require a lot more labor than would a simple redecoration, they are a lot less work than a complete renovation. See the Bibliography for more in-depth source books on the topic.

Another, simpler, way to make your bathroom a more convenient place is to change the fittings. You could install a new sink faucet, for example (make sure it fits the holes left by the old one), or add a personal shower, either one that adjusts vertically or one that can be detached and held in the hand. This fixture is useful for all kinds of things, from washing animals to bathing small children and people with disabilities, and it's also great for cleaning the tub. Placed in its holder, it functions as a normal showerhead.

Bathroom

A. *Ideally there should be a two-and-a-half-foot minimum in front of each bathroom fixture.*

B. *The toilet should not be visible from the door of the bathroom.*

C. *A full-length mirror can be mounted opposite the medicine cabinet mirror for grooming.*

D. *A wall-mounted magazine rack by the toilet is a nice touch, as is the reading light above the toilet.*

E. *Since soap dishes and towel bars located near tubs and showers are often used as grab bars, make sure they are designed and mounted to meet the same requirements as a grab bar, or install grab bars.*

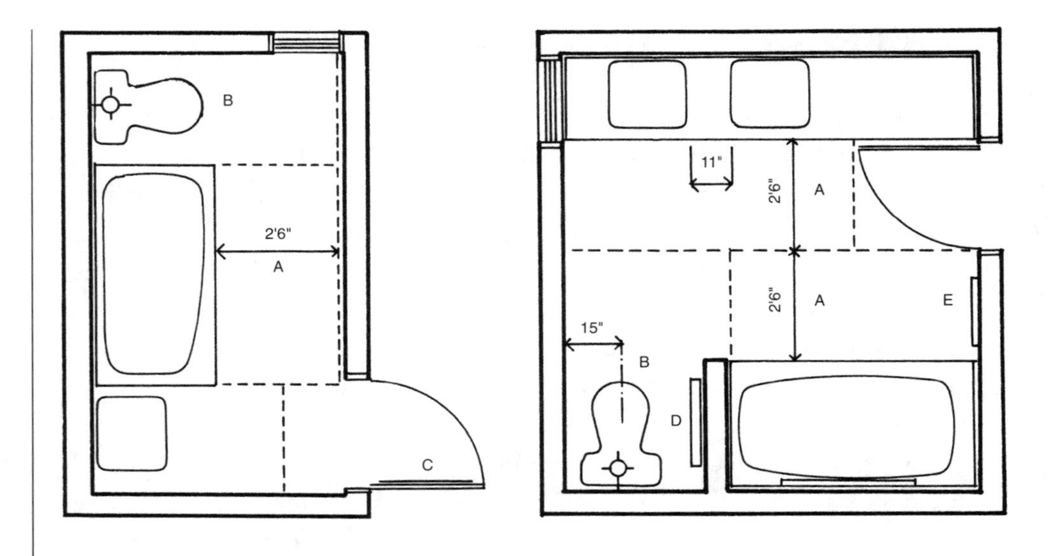

DECORATIVE FINISHES AND ACCESSORIES

There are many things you can do to give your bathroom a quick facelift. For example, thanks to its high level of humidity, the bathroom is a great place to keep plants if you have enough light. The traditional spot for a houseplant is the windowsill, but you could also group several small pots on a tray, a table, or a plant stand or hang large plants from the ceiling. Choose sturdy favorites, such as spider plants, aspidistra, philodendron, and sansevieria.

If you dislike the color of your existing wall tile, you can paint over it with yacht or marine paint. This must be done carefully and obviously won't look the same as replacing the tile, but it does make for a change. The surface must then be maintained with nonabrasive cleaners. Another option is to cover the existing tile with "green board," waterproof plasterboard or laminate sheets, which is less expensive than retiling but may not appeal to everyone's taste.

If your tile color is fine but you feel it's rather dull, apply new paint or vinyl-coated wallpaper to the untiled portions of the walls. If you choose a deep, dramatic, shiny color, it will result in a whole new look. Dark, shiny colors make small rooms seem larger—it's an optical effect similar to mirroring the entire room but kinder to one's personal vanity.

Another tried-and-true way to give a bathroom a whole new look is to paint the walls white and put washable white cotton rugs or acrylic carpeting on the floor; together with plants, this results in a fresh, airy look. For a country-style bath you could pleat or shirr printed fabric on a rod and hang it across the front of the sink enclosure (removing the doors, if any) as well as across the fronts of shelves. You can achieve a similar effect on a pedestal sink by using Velcro tape rather than a rod; glue one of the Velcro strips to the sink and sew the other to the shirred fabric. The fabric could match or coordinate with window curtains.

The use of towels in general is a quick way to give the bathroom a new look. They can be matched or contrasted with other accessories, such as glasses or cups, soap dishes, tissue holders, and shower curtains. If the wall covering or window treatment incorporates a variety of colors, you could have a few sets of towels that coordinate. In a plain room you might prefer patterned towels. Bright colors are a good choice for a child's bath.

Towels that are in good shape except for frayed edges can be given a new lease on life by adding a border of braid, bias tape, or fringe to the edges in a matching or contrasting color. This is fairly easy for anyone to do and will jazz up the whole room. The same trim can be added to curtains as well. You could even have a small chair (wicker or cane is a good, easy-care choice) with terrycloth-covered cushions trimmed in the same fashion.

Create a luxurious feeling with nice accessories. Keep small soaps, bath salts, or cotton balls in decorative glass jars, display your pretty bottles of perfume or cologne on a shelf in the bathroom, and keep the personal clutter of toiletries and makeup out of sight (see the section on storage, below, for more information). A good place to spend money is on coordinated accessories, such as a waste basket, tissue holder, lotion or liquid soap dispenser, and shelving. The coordinated effect will have a big impact in making your bathroom seem neater.

If a bathroom is used by more than one person or by a whole family, keeping clutter under control and maintaining a civilized atmosphere in the bathroom is difficult. Use semigloss or high-gloss enamel paint in a family bathroom rather than fabric and wall covering—it's easier to care for and keep looking good. Add as much storage as possible. Color-coordinate items such as towels, plastic cups, washcloths, and so on, with one color for each person, or whatever system makes sense to you. This will look cheerful and coordinated.

STORAGE

Many things must be stored in the bathroom, including prescription medications, soap, toothpaste, grooming aids, shampoo, cleaning aids, toilet paper, towels, and washcloths. You can't just leave them all sitting on the rim of the sink or tub, as it looks messy and can be unsafe. Each person using the room should have a special storage area, whether it's a whole shelf or just a section of the medicine cabinet.

In order to gain more space, you can replace your medicine cabinet with a larger one or add a second one. If this isn't possible, you can add roll-out shelves or bins below the sink and install extra shelves and cabinets wherever possible. Suggested spots include the back of the door, the inside of vanity doors, above the door, across the window, or on one wall of the tub or shower (for items that can get wet).

Towels are another prominent feature of the bathroom, particularly if it is small. You'll need a minimum of two feet of towel rack space for each person using the room. If you don't have enough space, put up hooks instead. A towel hung on a hook doesn't look as neat as one folded and hung over a bar, but it doesn't look nearly as bad as one that ends up on the floor because of lack of space.

Another aspect of bathroom storage is display shelving. If you like to read in the tub, you might want a small bookshelf or magazine rack in the bathroom; the shelf could also show off a small collection of decorative items (made of materials not affected by dampness).

OTHER USES

If your bathroom is big enough, you might want to use part of it as a dressing room or an exercise room. To turn a bathroom into a dual-purpose dressing room and bath, at minimum you'll need to find space for clothing storage (a wardrobe, closet, or chest of drawers), a full-length mirror, a makeup counter, and a chair to sit in while applying makeup or putting on shoes and socks. You'll want to add proper lighting too, for makeup and dressing (see the section on lighting, page 149, and Chapter 10, "The Bedroom," for more information).

To make a bathroom do double duty as an exercise room, you'll need to add the exercise equipment of your choice, such as an exercise bike, a treadmill, a stair-climbing machine, weights, an exercise mat, and maybe even a small television and VCR to watch instructional tapes. You'll also need a place to store all of the equipment neatly when not in use. A full-length mirror or even a mirrored wall is helpful to ensure that you maintain the right form while exercising.

EXERCISES

1. Who uses the bathroom? Do you need to provide for the special needs of young children or elderly persons? How do you accommodate overnight guests? What needs to be improved?

2. Is there enough storage? Do you have a place to store unattractive items out of sight?

3. Is your ideal bath bright and sunny or cozy and softly lit? Would a new color scheme help to achieve your preferred ambiance?

12

CHILDREN'S ROOMS

A child's room usually serves many purposes, from being a private domain to a multiuse play area. Ideally it is a special place, one where children can enjoy themselves with friends, siblings, and parents yet also be able to shut out the world and spend time in imaginative play. Among the activities that might take place in a child's room are studying, doing hobbies, listening to music, sleeping, dressing, and playing games, all of which happen in a limited space. Decorating such a room can be challenging yet fun. Although you do have to fit a lot of things into one place, deciding how to decorate this room provides an opportunity for you and your child to work together and indulge your imaginations.

The key elements of a successful child's bedroom are adequate and acceptable storage space; a well-lit, convenient study, work, and hobby area; and a comfortable, spacious play area; as well as someplace to sleep and perhaps space for a friend to stay overnight. Materials, finishes, and furniture should be sturdy and hard-wearing.

The nature of room decoration depends on the age of the child. Little children love small, cozy spaces and the sensation of having their own private place. They like to be able to look at and show off their collections of things, so provide plenty of shelf space. They also deserve a safe environment. You may want to consider adding bars to the windows (vertical bars no more than five inches apart are the standard). Also eliminate trailing electrical wires that a child might trip over, and place covers over unused electrical outlets.

In addition to privacy, teenagers need to feel that they have some control over their environment. They should be allowed to participate in decorating their own rooms as much as possible. At least let them choose their own scheme from several possibilities. A teenager's room might have an extra bed (for sleepover guests or for visitors to sit on); a worktable, desk, and dressing table area with a chair; plenty of storage space; and a full-length mirror. Remember, lots of fabric deadens sound, so teens should be encouraged to express their creativity with wall hangings, quilts, pillows, and curtains.

Use the suggestions and techniques given in the first three chapters for planning space, selecting colors and styles, and coordinating all of the various elements of a new decorating scheme. Combine these with the information in

CHECKLIST

1. Have you measured the room and made a floor plan?
2. Have you allowed your child to express his or her ideas about decorating the room?
3. Have you chosen a color scheme, incorporating your child's input as much as possible?
4. Do you have an evacuation plan in case of fire?
5. Are the light switches within the child's reach?
6. Is there enough room to store toys, clothing, and books?
7. Have you decided what furniture to buy?
8. Have you chosen safe, durable, nontoxic materials?

this chapter on the specific problems and details of decorating a child's room and you should be all set.

ADAPTABILITY/ADJUSTABILITY

Although little children love things made to their scale, such as lilliputian furniture, low doors and windows, and "secret passages" that adults don't fit through, they are constantly growing out of them, so keep adaptability in mind when buying child-size furniture or planning built-ins. One way to scale down the room is to hang such things as mirrors, wall clocks, bulletin or chalk boards, and posters at a child's eye level. These can then be moved up as the child grows.

Simple, functional designs that can be adjusted as the child grows are best—a storage unit with adjustable shelves, for example, or a desktop on legs that can be raised or replaced. Limit the purchase of child-size pieces to just a few, such as a table and chairs. Two or three small-scale pieces will please the child without blowing your budget. Everything else—beds, dressers, built-in furniture, or shelving—should be suitable for an adult-size person.

Since the bed is probably the biggest piece of furniture in the room, it's a good place to start thinking ahead. After all, a small child thinks bunk beds are neat; a teen might rather sleep in the bathtub. But a full-size bunk bed set that later can be taken apart and used as twin beds will please both ages. One great advantage with bunk beds is that the upper bunk, if not in nightly use by the room's resident, can be used for storage.

Other possibilities include loft beds, which free up floor space and can help to create intriguing decorative possibilities. The area underneath can be used for many purposes, including display, storage, or study space. Loft beds are available in lots of different styles, from simple to elaborate, and can be purchased ready-made (in which case they are removable) or built in place as a permanent fixture. Platform beds offer the option of useful storage or display space underneath. For overnight visitors there are child-size flip chairs and sofas that unfold into solid foam floor mattresses, as well as futons that fold up into sofas or can be rolled up and stored until needed.

STORAGE

Always aim for maximum storage in a child's room—you'll need more than you think. You might even want to cover an entire wall with shelving and closets. Children like to have lots of things in their possession, from toys to books to model kits to cassettes to collections of rocks or shells. They also enjoy being able to see what they have, so open storage will please them most. Try for an inexpensive, flexible system, such as adjustable shelving.

Plastic "milk crate" storage bins come in many different colors and sizes and can be used as a quick, easy place for kids to stash frequently used possessions. Portable bins on wheels and under-bed storage boxes can all take advantage of unused space without taking up precious play area. Unusual storage intrigues children and helps make the chore of putting things away a little more interesting. Try hanging string bags on pegs, like tiny hammocks. Place them low, within the child's reach.

Many of these storage options can be useful for getting dirty laundry out of sight too. In the closet you could hang a laundry bag low, within a child's reach, or place a child-size clothes hamper on the floor. You could also try using one of the "fun" laundry bags, in the shape of a giant doll or a dinosaur, to encourage your child to put dirty clothes in the proper place. Some laundry hamper systems, such as the type that uses brightly colored mesh bags supported on a framework of plastic pipe, can be converted for use as toy storage. These systems are inexpensive, come in both full-size and child-size versions, and allow kids to pick out their favorite colors.

For clothing storage, it's a simple matter to hang a rod below the existing rod in the closet, at a child's height, so that children can hang up their own clothes. You can also get small-size shoe racks and tiny hangers.

Modular furniture is a good choice for storage because it combines adaptability with good use of space. Thirty-inch-high units or open shelving, drawers, and cabinets can be set side by side or stacked, depending on the space available and the child's age (as he gets taller, so can the shelves). The base units can also be used to support tabletops (such as hollow-core flush doors or laminate tops) to create a custom work and hobby area for kids. You can even get a custom-colored or custom-shaped unit (companies that make cabinetry and countertops for kitchens should be able to supply laminate tops). Such units can start out as a study area and later become a hobby area or dressing table.

Storage can do double duty. A chest for toys can be topped with a cushion and used as a bench or window seat. A captain's bed is a kind of platform bed that has drawers beneath. A wall-hung cabinet can be faced with a mirror, chalkboard, or corkboard.

FLOORING

Children like being on the floor, which means it should be a comfortable place. A combination of hard surface—such as vinyl tile, sheet flooring, or polyurethane-coated hardwood—with area rugs or carpeting is best. You want the floor to be cushiony but also easy to clean, so washable area rugs are a better choice than wall-to-wall carpeting. To prevent accidents, make sure rugs are put down over nonskid matting or stuck down with double-face carpet tape.

Another possibility is to construct a special "play rug" of sheet vinyl flooring or cut-up carpet remnants that can be taken up when the child grows older. Such a rug might be decorated with educational motifs, such as the alphabet.

LIGHTING

As much as possible, natural light and ventilation are best in a child's room. It's a good idea to have lights on separate circuits, especially if two children share a room, so that one occupant can have a light on in one part of the room while it's dim in another. A dimmer on the main fixture can substitute for a night-light. Do-it-yourselfers might want to move the wall light switch down within a child's reach—a fairly simple change that can be reversed after the child has grown. An alternative is extenders. One type has two strings or cords hanging down, one for on, one for off. The other type looks like an elongated wall switch with switches at both top and bottom.

Otherwise children's rooms have the same lighting requirements as other bedrooms—a good reading light near the bed, a task light in the study area, and adequate lighting by the mirror and dressing table.

CREATIVE DISPLAYS

Once all of the practical considerations (study and hobby area, play space, and storage) are worked out, it's time to start thinking about decor. Kids like to be able to change things around and to put up their own decorations, like drawings they've made or posters featuring favorite cartoon characters or celebrities. It's a good idea, if possible, to finish one wall as a giant bulletin board or give it a surface that can be drawn on. There are special paint finishes that will turn a wall into a giant marker board. You can also buy four-by-eight-foot sheets of smooth white tileboard, which is like paneling, for this purpose. It wipes clean.

Horizontal surfaces should be low and broad, to display collections, toys, models, books, even a pet hamster's cage. It's easier for children to keep things

neat if storage is handy, so you can save yourself a lot of nagging by providing plenty of shelves as well as lift-top bins and chests.

Bright colors and fun textures are among the things children like best. Subdued good taste is not necessary in children's rooms—young children don't appreciate it. Even if your kids choose items that seem outrageous or silly to you, remember that it's their room.

Children's interests and tastes will change as they grow older, so try to keep the room decoration flexible. The Sesame Street theme so appealing at age four will not go over big at eight or ten. It's easier and cheaper to buy new sheets than to repaint the walls or throw out the furniture.

ACTIVITY AREAS

School-age children should have well-defined areas for work and play. A large, well-lit tabletop or an adjustable-height desk is especially useful because kids can keep using it as they get older. If your child likes to make things or do art projects, a large work area is particularly important.

Even if there is a play area in another part of your home, such as a family room or basement playroom, your child will want to play in his or her own room because it is such a personal place. Even in a small room, it's a good idea to leave as much floor space as possible. Keep the furniture in the room to a minimum or choose pieces that can be pushed out of the way. Or build a play loft if the ceiling height permits; forty-eight inches is adequate space for a child's loft. Kids love to climb a ladder to a secret hiding place. A closet is another great place to set up a secret castle.

SHARING A ROOM

When a room is shared it's important that the space be divided up so that each child has a private area for study or hobbies, individual storage space, and a dressing area, in addition to his or her own bed. You can use various elements to divide a room, from built-in partitions to sliding screens, heavy curtains, or a storage wall with shelves and closets. Both areas should get as much light as possible, so keep this in mind when choosing a divider. If only one part of the shared room has windows, the divider should be translucent or open enough to admit light.

Another way to promote the privacy of children who share a room is to use furnishings such as low bookshelves or a flip sofa as a movable divider. In a small room movable dividers give children the option of playing in a single large space or closing the divider for more privacy.

WORKING WITH YOUR CHILD

How much should your child be involved in decorating? As much as possible. You, as an adult, should make the practical decisions about storage and display, lighting, and safety. But children around seven or eight really want to be part of the decision-making process. At the very least they should be allowed to choose their own color scheme. Even if they pick a really peculiar color or combination of colors, try to compromise rather than just telling them no. Let them choose between furniture styles in the same price range as well as fabric patterns and storage items. (See the exercise in Chapter 1, "Child's Personal Inventory," page 22 for more details on this topic.)

EXERCISES

1. How old are your children? How can their current furnishings be adapted as they grow older? What will have to be replaced?

2. Make a list of the activities that will be taking place in the bedroom (check all that apply).

   _____ Arts and crafts
   _____ Play activities (building blocks, board games, puppet theater, puzzles)
   _____ Studying and school projects
   _____ Reading
   _____ Working on a computer
   _____ Dancing or exercising
   _____ Playing an instrument
   _____ Listening to music
   _____ Entertaining friends
   _____ Talking on the telephone
   _____ Watching videotapes or TV
   _____ Other

   How have you provided for these activities in your room plan?

3. What collections and other special possessions will your child want to keep in his or her room? Can some of them be kept in another place, such as the play area of a family room?

4. Do two children have to share a room? Are they close in age and have similar interests? How do you plan to accommodate their differences?

5. Does your child have any special requirements, such as allergies or physical or learning disabilities? (See the Bibliography for further information on decorating a room for a child with special needs.)

Keep in mind that children of all ages like to get involved in the decoration of their own personal spaces. Make a copy of these exercises and give them to your child, if he or she is old enough to read. Better yet, make a copy for each of you and go down the list together, creating joint responses. Your child may have some crazy ideas (at least they may seem that way to you), but don't dismiss them immediately—upon further thought you may find that these off-the-wall notions can be translated into wacky but highly practical decorating details. Children love to play with color, so you might want to put together a set of paint chips and fabric or tile samples for them to have as their own. An older child, particularly a teen, may enjoy helping you draw room plans and create color charts for other rooms as well.

13

HOBBY AND LAUNDRY ROOMS

HOBBY ROOM

You don't have to be a professional carpenter or a skilled craftsperson to justify the use of a separate room for your hobby, whether it be sewing, woodworking, or watercolors. In a workroom, studio, or workshop, you can finally get your projects organized and completed. And a hobby room doesn't have to take up a lot of space; you don't even need a whole room. You can adapt whatever space you have, whether it's a corner of the garage, basement, or laundry room. Even a large closet will do.

If your chosen activity is something noisy and messy, like woodworking, which generates a lot of sawdust and other trash, you might want to put it in the garage or the basement, away from the living areas. If your hobby involves using paint or solvents that generate noxious vapors, you need good ventilation. If you're going to be moving equipment and materials in and out, a space with its own entrance (again, the garage or basement) is the best choice.

You can also combine a hobby area or workshop with a laundry room, since most of the requirements for both are in place—countertops, work space, electrical outlets, and good lighting and ventilation. It really depends on the kind of activities taking place. A laundry room is a fine place to repot plants or wrap gifts; it may not be such a great place for decorative painting or working with clay.

Before you begin, consult Chapter 1, "Developing an Overall Plan," for suggestions on how to plan a room efficiently. Then read this chapter to discover more specific hints on how to plan a hobby or laundry room, or a combination of the two.

ORGANIZATION AND STORAGE

For a home workshop or hobby room, you'll need a work area—which can be anything from a tabletop to the space that your loom or easel occupies—or a workbench, depending on the type of activities that will be taking place. Workroom organization is like kitchen organization: you want to be able to find everything easily and not have to walk around too much. Tools and materials, from scissors to paintbrushes and yarn to clay, should be kept near their point of

CHECKLIST

1. Have you measured the room or area available and made a floor plan?
2. Have you chosen a color scheme?
3. Have you chosen decorating materials that will resist moisture?
4. Is the lighting adequate for each of the space's uses?
5. Is the wiring adequate for use of large appliances or power tools, if these will be used?
6. Do you have sufficient storage?
7. Do you have a high, locked cupboard for storage of dangerous or poisonous materials?
8. Do you have sufficient tabletop or counter space for seasonal activities that will likely take place in your hobby room, such as cutting and arranging flowers or wrapping gifts?

use. Small tools, especially those that you use frequently, can be hung on the wall for easy access or kept neatly organized and at hand in a container on top of your work surface. Tools that you use less frequently can be stored in bins or drawers below the work surface. You can also group equipment according to task, with certain types of tools (for plumbing, painting, or sewing, for example) all in the same place.

For an informal look, pegboard is serviceable and inexpensive for wall storage of tools and implements. By painting the pegboard white and tracing the outline of each tool where it hangs, you can easily return each one to its proper place and keep everything well organized. If you want to spend more money for better-looking storage, there are plenty of wall storage systems to choose from. The vinyl-coated wire systems that can be found at most housewares stores are versatile. They provide several different types of storage, from shelves to baskets to turntables, in a single system. You can also put narrow shelves on the backs of doors and hang baskets from the ceiling to create more storage space. Lumber or large items, such as folding easels, can be stored between ceiling joists if your workroom is set up in a garage, attic, or basement.

Some hobbies, such as knitting or needlework, require relatively little space, both for the activity itself and for the materials that need to be stored. If you are a knitter you may be fine with a large basket and part of a closet or storage unit to call your own, as long as both are neatly organized. Other crafts, such as weaving or pottery, take up a good deal more space. Weavers require space for a loom, materials, and completed projects. Potters need access to water, room for a wheel, and proper storage to prevent clay from drying out. They may also need to store glazes and to accommodate a kiln.

Model makers will need to store both miniature tools and other items ranging from the merely small to the minuscule. While they don't take up much space, small items, such as those used to re-create miniature rooms, need carefully organized storage. See-through plastic boxes or glass jars with lids are one solution.

Whatever your chosen hobby or leisure time activity, one thing is an absolute must: anything potentially harmful or poisonous, from solvents to needles to drill bits, should be locked in a cabinet out of the reach of small children if there is any chance they will be present.

LAUNDRY ROOM

If you're starting from scratch you'll have to find the space for your laundry room or area and then organize it. The laundry area can be located in a number of places besides the basement or a separate utility room. Even a closet or hallway will work as long as there is access to plumbing and electrical or gas connections (for a gas dryer). The home laundry can be near the kitchen, bathroom, basement, or bedrooms. Some washers and dryers are now designed to fit in closets and other small spaces; there are also special stacked washer-dryer units as well as portable washers that can be rolled out of a corner or closet and hooked up to the sink. Both are ideal for apartment dwellers. There's also a case to be made for locating the laundry room upstairs or wherever the bedrooms are. This is more convenient than the traditional basement or kitchen location because it's where the dirty clothes and linens usually originate.

Among the useful items that might be incorporated in a laundry room are a fold-down ironing board, storage cupboards, sorting bins, a separate bin for clothes that will be dry-cleaned, a clothing rod or rack for hanging clothes, and a drying rack (for drying hand laundry or clothes that don't go in the dryer).

What else might you want to use the room for? Think of other activities that need a place of their own. Wrapping gifts, for example, sometimes has to be done in secret, so the laundry room is a good place to store wrapping paper, ribbons, scissors, boxes, and tape. It might also be the perfect place to store pet supplies (giant bags of dry food or cat litter, carriers, and leashes) as well as cleaning supplies, chemicals and poisons (in a locked cupboard if you have children), shoe-care supplies, vases and materials for flower arranging, tools for minor repairs, small sports equipment, camping equipment, and emergency supplies, such as candles. If the laundry is also the mudroom, as it is in many houses, it might be a place for coat hooks and a boot shelf.

When designing your laundry room, keep in mind the following requirements. For the washer you will need a means to catch accidental overflow. This can be either a floor drain tied into the washer drainpipe or a floor pan with no drain that goes under the washer to collect minor drips. For the dryer you will need to vent the heat and humidity. In a traditional laundry room, place the dryer against an exterior wall so it can be vented easily. If the laundry area has no exterior wall, you can route the vent through the walls, ceiling, or floor to the outside as long as the distance doesn't exceed the twenty to twenty-five feet recommended by most manufacturers. A lint basket is an alternative to an exterior vent. The drawbacks are that it must be cleaned frequently and it captures only lint; humidity and odors stay in the room. If you live in an apartment building, check the local laws about venting.

Flooring

Hard floors such as concrete wear the best. Concrete must be sealed to prevent dust. You could also install hard-wearing vinyl tile or sheet flooring. Local building codes often specify that laundry room floors be covered in vinyl.

Of course, hard floors are hard on your feet, so if you have to do a lot of standing in front of a piece of equipment, whether an ironing board or a table saw, put a washable rubber or foam-backed mat there. Your feet and back will be grateful. These materials have the added advantage of providing a safe, nonslip surface, a particularly good idea in the laundry room.

If the room you're using has a wood floor, you probably will want to protect it with a vinyl "rug" or other hard-wearing material. Of course, any hobby that creates dust or other debris needs flooring that can be wiped or mopped, such as vinyl sheeting or tile. And although an area rug provides a note of color and softness in a sewing room, it's also a good place to lose pins, needles, and other small notions, so any rug you choose should have a low pile and a subdued pattern.

LIGHTING AND VENTILATION

Windows and skylights are good sources of light and ventilation in the workroom or laundry room, but there are other options as well. If there is no operable window in the space and you need ventilation, you can install an exhaust fan with a spark-proof motor in an exterior wall or roof. Lighting can come from fluorescent shop lights, available in four- and eight-foot lengths. This style of lighting gives even, shadowless light and also uses less electricity than do incandescent fixtures, although it can be aesthetically unattractive. One eight-foot or two four-foot fixtures give enough lighting for a hundred square feet of floor space. The least expensive form of task lighting comes from clamp-on lamps, which can be moved from place to place if necessary. Another possibility is portable halogen work lights, which give bright, clear illumination and can be stashed away when not needed. Be advised that these lights give off a lot of heat and must be fitted with a glass shade to block UV radiation. Alternatively you can install under-shelf fluorescent lights to provide illumination. If you paint the walls white or a light color, you'll get more light through reflection.

Consult an electrician about wiring. If you use portable power tools, such as a drill or jigsaw, you'll need several 110-volt outlets. Ideally these should be wired to a dedicated 20-amp circuit separate from the lighting. Large power equipment, such as a table saw, may require another separate 110-volt circuit of higher amperage or a 220-volt circuit. A washing machine uses a standard 120-volt electrical outlet on a 20-amp circuit, while an electric dryer requires 240 volts on a 50-amp circuit. A gas-powered dryer needs a three-quarter-inch supply pipe and a 120-volt, 20-amp outlet to run the motor.

An outlet strip along the edge of your work area can be very useful for plugging in power tools. A retractable extension cord is another useful option.

EXERCISES

1. First make a list of the projects, hobbies, or repairs you do most frequently (potting plants, mending china, antiquing picture frames, making furniture). How much storage and work space does each require?

____

____

____

____

____

____

____

____

2. Determine the available space. Do a survey of your home and really think about what's available to you and what you want to do with the space.

3. What is your dream hobby space like? Make a list of the special features it would have as well as all of the tools and materials you would like to store in it. Compare this list of wants and needs to the space you have available and see how many features you can incorporate.

____

____

____

____

____

____

____

4. Here is a checklist of items for an ideal laundry room:

_____ Washer and dryer
_____ Sink
_____ Fold-down, wall-mounted ironing board
_____ Storage space
_____ Bins for sorting clothes into light, dark, and delicate
_____ Separate bin for dry-clean-only clothing
_____ Surface area for folding clothing
_____ Hanging rod for ironed clothing
_____ Rack for air-drying clothing

PART THREE

✦ ✦ ✦ ✦

SPECIFICS

KULTURENS GRYNING

14

FURNITURE AND FURNISHINGS

Care in the selection of furniture is important for several obvious reasons. First, as the largest objects in a room, furniture has a major visual impact. Second, for most of us it constitutes a major expenditure. Finally, most likely that sofa, armoire, or dining table you buy is something you will live with for a long time, so you want to make sure it is the right one for you.

SHOPPING TIPS

The factors you need to consider when buying furniture include appearance and style; size (is it in scale with the room and with your other furniture?); suitability (will the piece fit in with your way of life and the activities that take place in the room?); and quality, including the quality of both the materials and the method of construction.

Furniture should be comfortable and durable or it's not worth buying. The occasional wooden side chair may be bought as sculpture, but you shouldn't spend a lot on it. See the following sections on case goods and upholstered furniture for tips on determining quality and comfort.

When you venture out into the furniture marketplace, you will find yourself faced with a plethora of choices. Generally, both upholstered pieces and case goods (wood furniture) can be divided into two style categories: contemporary and traditional. Within both categories you can find original pieces, reproductions, and adaptations of classic designs. What you buy will be determined by your personal taste and budget. You really can't go wrong with classics; after all, they have survived the test of time. In adapted form they may be better suited to modern interiors and lifestyles. If your taste runs to the avant-garde and you can afford it, go ahead and buy original, cutting-edge furniture designs. They are the antiques and collector's items of tomorrow.

Shopping should be a patient, pragmatic endeavor. Make a list of the furniture sources in your area and take a tour to become familiar with what they offer. It's also a good idea to check out furniture stores in other areas, perhaps when you are traveling, to see what they have to offer and to shop for small items, such as accent pieces. Possible sources, in addition to furniture specialty stores, include design centers, auction rooms, and secondhand furniture stores. It's also a good idea to check out the retail branches of the stylish houseware and furniture stores springing up around the country, including the large import stores and those featuring ready-to-assemble pieces. Many of these stores also issue catalogs, which are a boon if there are no outlets in your area.

Develop the habit of always checking the prices of furniture in shops and at flea markets, sales, and auction rooms—that way, when it is time to buy, you'll have a clear idea of the going rate. Then, when you can't stand your old sofa one minute longer, you won't end up spending twice as much as you have to.

Another source is the mail-order outlet that sells factory-fresh, brand-name furniture for up to 50 percent off the suggested retail price. Buying furniture at a discount is extremely satisfying if you get a great deal on something you really like. These outlets don't carry every model by every manufacturer, but they are worth checking into. When you find the piece you want at a local retailer, note how much it costs and get the model number, finish, fabric style, and size. Also ask how long delivery will take. Then call an outlet for a price quote. Be sure to

CHECKLIST

If you can answer yes to all of the following questions, you are probably ready to go ahead and purchase furniture.

1. Have you decided on which pieces of furniture you need?
2. Have you determined your budget?
3. Have you established your furniture priorities?
4. Have you thought about ways to reuse or refurbish furniture you already own?
5. Have you measured the relevant areas where furniture is to go?
6. Have you decided on a color scheme?
7. Have you considered buying accent pieces or displaying those you already have?
8. Have you determined how your furniture pieces will fit into your overall plan?

ask how much sales tax, shipping, and insurance will be added to the cost of the item so that you can make a direct comparison. Once you have ordered the piece, you usually receive a confirmation on your order by mail, with a bill for half the cost of the piece. The balance is due on delivery, which may take as long as ninety days. Only you can decide if the money you save is worth the wait for a new armchair or coffee table.

Since you're probably paying a lot of money for an item, even at a discount, be sure to find out what happens if the item arrives damaged or if, once it's in your living room, you decide you don't like it. Before making your purchase, it's a good idea to check with the Mail Order Action Line of the Direct Marketing Association (11 West 42nd Street, P.O. Box 3861, New York, NY 10163-3861) and the Better Business Bureau in the town where the firm is based to see if there are any complaints about it on file.

See page 259 for a list of well-regarded discount furniture retailers you can contact for brochures or catalogs. Whatever you buy, make it the best you can afford.

CASE GOODS

Case goods is the term used in the furniture industry for all nonupholstered furniture, including chairs, tables, desks, and cabinets of all types, as well as benches and settles. Case goods can be made of metal, plastic, wood, even marble, or a combination of these. In general, the cost of a piece should be determined by the quality of the materials and workmanship that went into it. The difference in the price of two apparently similar pieces of furniture may be determined by the finishing processes, hand labor, and materials that went into constructing the piece. Any kind of hand-finishing process will add to the cost of a piece of furniture (and should add to its value as well).

The most expensive materials used in furniture construction include domestic hardwoods, such as maple, walnut, oak, pecan, cherry, and birch, as well as tropical hardwoods, such as mahogany and teak. If you buy furniture made from these woods, check to be sure they were harvested from plantations, not from environmentally endangered sources. The manufacturer's label should make it clear where the wood comes from. If not, don't buy the furniture.

Softwoods like pine, cedar, and fir cost less than hardwoods. Even less expensive are wood substitutes, such as particleboard and hardboard. Particleboard (or chipboard, a similar material) is usually covered with a veneer, which may be of hardwood or plastic laminate. Hardboard, on the other hand, is often embossed with a wood grain pattern and finished to look like real wood.

Veneer has a bad reputation, but improvements in adhesives and manufacturing techniques ensure that a well-made piece from a reputable manufacturer should have no problems with cracking or peeling and should last almost as long as the same piece made of solid hardwood. In fact, since veneer construction consists of several layers of wood cross-banded for strength, it may last even longer.

Some case goods may be advertised as having "solid wood construction." This means that all of the exposed parts of a piece of furniture are made of solid wood. Interior parts, however, may be of particleboard or other materials. Check the label or hang tag to see what the story is. Let the salesperson explain the materials and construction, but don't rely on his or her avowal of quality. Gather the information and rely on your own judgment based on research. Here are some tests you can do yourself:

✦ High-quality case goods should be sturdy, well made, and stable. Drawers should not stick, legs should not wobble, and hardware should be attached tightly. The finish should be even, without nicks, spots, or streaks (unless part of the design).

✦ Turn the piece over or look underneath to see how the different parts are joined together. Where the legs join the top or seat of the piece, the joint should be reinforced with a corner block. Where screws are used to join pieces together, there should be washers to protect the wood. Look at joints to make sure they are tight, as any gaps will cause swaying or squeaking.

✦ Test to see if joints are stable. Put your hands on a table or cabinet and rock it gently. It should not wobble or creak. Sit in a chair and sway gently from side to side; it too should not wobble or make noise. Still seated, push on the arms and back; there should be no give. Feel under the edge of a tabletop or chair seat to see if the surfaces are smooth. This is another sign of workmanship. The leaves of an extension table should match the rest of the top in terms of color, graining, and style. Be sure there is at least seven inches of clearance between your knees and the underside of a dining table when seated. Also check to see if there's room for the arms of a chair to fit beneath.

✦ If you want to check out a piece of storage furniture, such as a chest or cabinet, rap the top and sides with your knuckles to see how solid the construction is. Thin panels will have a hollow sound, while heavy panels, which ensure solidity and strength, will sound dull. Also check the back: plywood and hardwood backs are sturdier than particleboard. Look at the drawers to make sure they slide out smoothly. Equal spacing around the drawer front is a sign of quality; there should not be more than one-quarter inch of play from side to side if you jiggle it. Take out the drawer and check for such details as built-in guides and stops (these may be of wood, metal, or plastic); tightly fitted joints (no glue drips should be visible); and dust panels between each drawer slot. All are signs of good quality. Cabinet doors should hang evenly and open smoothly. The hardware and hinges should be securely attached, with screws that go all the way through the panel and are anchored with a bolt and washer.

UPHOLSTERED FURNITURE

A sofa and accompanying armchairs serve as the centerpiece of most living room arrangements; therefore, they are an important purchase. Be sure to check the quality of the frame, springs, webbing, and cushioning material carefully.

With upholstered furniture, you get what you pay for. That five-hundred-dollar sofa (unless the price is the result of a deep discount) is not going to last as long or be as comfortable as its twelve-hundred-dollar counterpart. With upholstered pieces it's especially important to buy from a reputable source because you can't see the frame, filling, and springs. Remember that what's on display in a showroom is often not all there is; you can usually get a sofa or chair you like in a different fabric or size. Be sure to ask.

Kiln-dried hardwood is the best material for sofa and chair frames. You shouldn't hear creaks when you sit on the piece or try to lift it. Coil springs tied closely together provide the most comfortable support. Eight-way hand-tied springs (meaning they are tied together in eight different places) are the most durable. Wire-linked coil springs and arched sinuous springs (or S-springs) cost less and offer fairly comfortable seating.

Pocketed springs are the top choice for comfortable back cushions, while sinuous spring backs are less expensive. Usually, if the back cushions are loose, there are no springs in the back. Instead, webbing provides resilience. This type of construction is less expensive than attached cushions. Webbing should be four inches wide for the seat and three inches wide for the back. In general, high-quality examples of each type will be equal in comfort; webbing, however, is the least resilient. In many ways it's a matter of personal taste. Some prefer the firm resistance of spring backs, others think webbing is fine.

The most durable, comfortable foam for cushions is high-density polyurethane foam, which is wrapped with down, cotton batting, or synthetic fiberfill. Each wrap has its advantages. Down is softest, but it is also expensive and requires constant plumping and shaping. Cotton batting and synthetic fiberfill are firmer but keep their shape better, are comfortable, and give good value for the money.

Don't buy an upholstered piece without sitting on it first. Give it a "sit test": sit down on a sofa or chair to gauge its firmness and comfort. See if the arms and back are the right height, the seat dimensions are in proportion to your own, and there's enough support for your back. Buy it only if you are completely satisfied.

The upholstery itself should be of good-quality fabric and tailored with care. Check to see that the fabric fits smoothly over the piece and that the pattern repeats match. The welting (cording along seams) should be neatly sewn, and there should be no puckering or loose threads anywhere. The skirt, if present, should be lined and weighted to hang straight.

Upholstery fabrics get a lot of wear, so you should consider durability along with color and pattern. Leather and vinyl are easiest to care for and toughest, but one is expensive and the other is not suitable for formal rooms. Next in terms of durability come pile fabrics, such as velvet, corduroy, and plush. Flat, tightly woven fabrics, such as tapestries, satins, muslins, and tweeds, are next on the list. The more tightly woven they are, the better they will wear.

While natural fibers often feel better to the touch than synthetics, they are not as durable. Choosing a natural-synthetic blend gives you the best of both. Nylon adds toughness and helps a fabric last. Upholstery fabrics come treated with a soil- and stain-resistant finish, but you can always add a further treatment once you get it home.

BUYING USED FURNITURE

Buying used or secondhand furniture can be a great way to get a bargain, find an unusual piece, and do a favor for the environment. Sources for secondhand furniture include secondhand shops, junkyards, salvage shops, charity or thrift shops, and auctions. Wood or metal furniture is generally a better buy than upholstered furniture, as it is inherently more durable. Depending on your taste and resourcefulness, you may find that you can buy most of the furniture you need secondhand or at an auction.

The rules for quality in secondhand furniture are the same as for buying new. You will have to accept some wear, but it should not affect the usefulness of the piece or be disfiguring. Don't buy pieces that need extensive repair, refinishing, or reupholstering unless you are experienced at these jobs and know what you're getting into. On the other hand, if you're willing to spend money for professional work, some older pieces may still prove a great buy.

SLIPCOVERS

Slipcovers give you a lot of decorating possibilities for about half the cost of reupholstering. They can be used out of necessity, to cover outdated or threadbare upholstery, or they can be used to give furniture a different look from summer to winter and to increase the longevity of your existing upholstery.

Slipcovers can be loosely draped or tightly fitted; they can incorporate details such as welting, raised seams, tassels, ruffles, and bows, or they can combine two or more fabrics. Sturdy, washable upholstery cottons are probably the best choice, but since the cover for a large sofa probably won't fit in the washing machine, you might as well use a dry-clean-only fabric. Rayon velvet, for instance, wears well and gives an elegant look.

Finding someone to make slipcovers should not be difficult. Ask relatives, friends, and coworkers if they have had slipcovers made and if they can recommend someone. Many upholstery stores, decorating outlets, and fabric stores offer a slipcover-making service or can recommend a seamstress or tailor. Major department stores that have a furniture department may do custom slipcovers.

You can also check the yellow pages. It's always a good idea to check more than one source—you will almost undoubtedly save money. For example, many department stores subcontract their slipcover work to independent sources. You'll pay less if you eliminate the middleman.

Many vendors sell both materials and finished covers. Others will also work with material you have purchased from another source. Ask to see examples of their finished work. A well-made slipcover should have straight seams. The stitching should be neat, and the cover should fit the outline of the chair fairly closely. Finally, ask the vendor for references and check them.

UNFINISHED AND RTA FURNITURE

You are probably familiar with unfinished furniture stores, which offer basic wood pieces from bookshelves to desks and tables to bedframes, usually made of unfinished pine. Although these are often uninspired in terms of design, they're great for kids' rooms or bedrooms and you can stain or paint them to suit your taste.

RTA stands for ready to assemble. This type of furniture is often sold by mail order, since the disassembled pieces are shipped flat in a carton ("knocked down," often abbreviated as KD) and you put them together at home. RTA furniture is also sold through home center stores, discount stores, and office supply stores. Examples of RTA furniture include TV/VCR trolleys, office file carts and printer stands, small side tables and stools, and modular wall systems. These may be of wood, metal, or plastic, or a combination of the three. RTA furniture varies in quality, so it's best to buy from a reputable supplier that offers nationally known brand names or from a manufacturer's mail-order catalog.

CUSTOM FURNITURE

If you can't find what you want in a retail store or at auction, you may want to try buying a custom-made piece to fit a special spot. If you don't want to spend the money for a commissioned piece, you can go to a craftsperson who specializes in reproductions or a furniture designer who offers a range of limited production pieces. Both options will cost less than a custom piece and you will still be able to acquire a beautifully made, sturdy, out-of-the-ordinary piece of furniture.

To find possible sources of such furniture, check interior design magazines and the home supplement of your local newspaper. City magazines may also carry ads for custom or limited-production furniture. *Vermont* magazine, for example, has a special section each year on craftspeople who live in the state. If there is a design center nearby, call to see if they allow nonprofessionals to browse in the showrooms. Many have relaxed their rules and permit members of the public not only to shop but to buy without the assistance of a decorator or architect.

EXERCISES

1. Make a master list of the pieces you want to buy and the prices you expect to pay. The list should detail which room each piece will go in and its approximate dimensions. Your list should be divided into essential pieces and furniture you'd like to add sometime in the future.

Piece	Price	Room	Dimensions	Essential	To Buy Over Time

2. Make a copy of the floor plan for each room where you intend to add furniture and annotate it with the details of the size and type of piece you want to buy.

3. Go through your portfolio of magazine clippings and pick out examples of upholstered furniture and case goods that appeal to you. If the magazine has a source guide, use it to find out where the piece might be obtained. Make a list here of the details.

Piece	Price	Color	Materials	Where Seen	Source

15

WINDOW TREATMENTS

Windows let the sun in and keep the wind and rain out. Just as the eyes are thought to be the mirrors of the soul, windows are the eyes of the home. Since they can be seen from the outside (and often allow people to see in), they are part of the public face of your home. The purpose of window treatments such as curtains, blinds, and shutters is threefold: to create privacy, to control light, and, last but not least, to complement the decorative scheme of the room.

WINDOW TYPES

The most common window is the multipane double-hung sash type, which is fairly easy to decorate. Other types include:

- Bay and bow windows, which project outward from your home and sometimes have a window seat or radiator below the sill
- Casement windows, which swing in or out on a side pivot
- Awning windows, which swing out from the bottom
- Hopper windows, which open at the top, essentially the opposite of awning types
- Jalousie windows, which have horizontal slats
- Picture windows, which consist of a single large, fixed pane
- Clerestory windows, which are small, narrow strip windows located near the ceiling
- Palladian windows, which are rounded at the top

Although they are not, strictly speaking, windows, French doors and sliding glass doors also may need curtains or blinds to control light and give privacy.

DRAPERIES AND CURTAINS

The terms are often used interchangeably, but technically draperies and curtains are not the same. Draperies cover the window completely when closed and frame it when open. They can be hung from a point at the top edge of the window frame or above it, all the way up to the ceiling cornice line. They may end at any point from the sill to the floor, but they are always at least as long as the window itself. They are usually fairly formal and are used in formal rooms such as the living room and dining room, but the actual degree of formality depends on the fabric used and whether embellishments such as valances, fringe, jabots, swags, and tiebacks are added.

Curtains hang closer to the window than draperies, inside the window frame. If they are made of sheer material, they may be referred to as sheers, glass curtains, or sash curtains. Curtains may hang to the sill (the bottom of the window molding) or to the floor. If tailored, they hang straight. Ruffled curtains are tied back.

Café curtains hang from rings on traditional metal café rods (see "Window Hardware," on page 206). They are hung in one tier across the bottom half of the window, which is the customary style adapted from the French cafés where they originated, or in two overlapping tiers to cover the entire window. These

CHECKLIST

1. Have you taken measurements? (If not, see the figure "Measuring Windows" later in this chapter.)
2. Are the windows in good condition? (Be sure to repaint, or replace cracked panes, if necessary, before installing new window treatments.)
3. Have you established a budget for your window treatments?
4. Have you considered remaking existing window treatments?
5. Have you considered light and privacy needs in designing new window treatments?
6. Will the new window treatment harmonize with your overall room scheme?
7. Have you thought about how your windows will appear from outside the house? Is this a concern?
8. Have you considered how to deal with any "problem" windows?

days, any curtain that is hung in one or two tiers is generally referred to as a café curtain, no matter what the style of heading (see below) or hardware may be.

Draperies and curtains may hang straight, as a panel, but they are far more often gathered or pleated. The different types of pleats are known as drapery or curtain headings and used to be achieved only by laborious hand sewing. Now, however, you can buy various heading tapes, which consist of fabric strips that have integral pockets and drawstrings. You purchase the tape by the yard and baste it onto the curtain or drapery fabric. Then you simply pull the drawstring to create the heading.

Pleated headings are the most formal. Various types of pleats include pinch pleats (also known as triple or French pleats), pencil pleats, box pleats, and goblet (cartridge) pleats, all of which have a very tailored appearance. Cased headings (also known as rod pocket headings) are simply gathered or shirred on the rod, which is threaded through a casing sewn into the top of the fabric. Scalloped headings may hang from metal or wooden rings or fabric tabs, which may be used with straight headings as well. For sources of information on how to make various types of curtain and drapery headings yourself, see the Bibliography.

WINDOW HEADINGS

Window headings function to hide hardware and the tops of curtains and draperies. They are a finishing touch and are useful when dealing with awkward or undistinguished windows to create the look of architectural detail where there is none.

A valance is fabric mounted on a backing of board or stiffened with buckram. Sometimes called a pelmet or lambrequin, a valance may be trimmed with fringe or braid. It is generally a formal, traditional style. A cornice is a wood or metal heading that conceals the top of the curtain or drape and the window hardware; it too is very formal. The great advantage of both of these types of headings is that they can be made in any shape, from scalloped to saw-toothed, or can imitate a classic architectural motif, such as a Gothic or Palladian arch. Sometimes a cornice is combined with a fabric heading.

Fabric headings are referred to generally as valances, specifically as festoons or swags. These are softer in effect than cornices. Festoons may be single, double, or triple and have tails (also known as jabots because they resemble that article of clothing) that hang down on both sides. Swags are festoons without tails and may be combined with pleats. They must be carefully shaped and tailored. Simple headings may be pleated or shirred and made of the same fabric as the curtains. They are more informal.

CHOOSING A STYLE

The window treatment you choose will be determined by a number of factors: the style of the room, the design of the window, and your budget. A period home or apartment with high ceilings and tall windows looks wonderful with lavish, elegantly draped and swagged windows, while crisp Roman shades might be better in a modern dwelling. Another consideration is that window treatments must leave the windows operable.

If the room is decorated fairly simply, a simple window treatment will balance the look. An elaborately decorated room, on the other hand, will look unfinished if the windows are left bare or with minimal curtains. If you want to keep your window treatments simple, use pale or muted colors and plain woven fabrics. A single strong color may work as well.

REQUIREMENTS OF DIFFERENT WINDOWS

Some windows hardly need curtains at all; they have handsome moldings, attractive proportions, look out onto a beautiful view, and get just the right amount of sun. Rarely will you encounter this ideal, but in general, a window with good moldings and proportions requires only a minimal treatment. A curtain or shade mounted within the casing and falling just to the sill, for example, will not detract from the window itself.

The size of the window is an important factor. Small windows should not be burdened with a lot of fabric, while tall windows are enhanced by elaborate draperies. The amount of space around the window is a factor too. You can use window treatments to solve problems of awkwardly placed or unattractive windows. For example, a series of small windows along a wall can be treated as a single unit by running a traverse rod along the wall at ceiling height and hanging a single panel or series of panels that can be drawn away from the windows to let in light during the day, then closed at night for privacy. Draperies that extend out beyond the window frame and down to the floor lend importance and proportion to a single small window smack in the middle of a wall.

There are other special situations that will influence the style of curtains or draperies used. Double windows can be treated as one window or two. Bay or bow windows can be dealt with in three different ways: (1) treat each section of the bay separately, (2) use a traverse rod or pole designed to fit around the bay, or (3) install a curtain rod straight across the front of the bay so it is closed off when the curtains are drawn. If a window adjoins a wall or a large piece of furniture on one side, you may not be able to use a pair of curtains or drapes; the best solution might be a shade or a single asymmetrical drapery. Recessed windows are another situation where shades are the best option. Shades also work well with window seats, as do sill-length curtains or drapes.

A radiator under a window calls for special treatment, as you don't want to block the heat with heavy curtains. One possible solution is to use a shade and hang dress draperies on either side of the window that fall on either side of the radiator. A shade and a decorative window heading are another good combination, as are simple sill-length curtains or draperies, depending on how much space there is between the window and the radiator.

EFFECTS OF DIFFERENT FABRICS

Sheer curtains can be useful in a number of situations. Not only do they have a light, unobtrusive look, but they are useful for blocking an unattractive view while still admitting light and for cutting glare in rooms that get a lot of late-afternoon sun. The best colors for sheers are white, cream, and very pale pastels in warm tones. Be careful with colors in sheers, as they tend to tint the sunlight coming through them. Choose a color that flatters your complexion as well as the room itself. Fabrics suitable for use as sheers include voile, lightweight muslin, and lace, all of which are available in easy-care synthetic fibers. Sheers can look romantic, crisp, or country-casual depending on how they are used.

They can be used alone or combined with a heavier drape, which may be desirable during winter.

If you want a grand effect, use fabrics such as brocades, paisleys, heavy silks, or taffeta in dark, rich colors and several layers (see "Choosing Fabrics" page 199, for a description of different fabrics). Layer a shade or glass panel with draperies over it and a valance or swag topping the whole thing. You don't have to spend a lot of money for this effect because it depends more on the amount of cloth than it does on the fabric itself, so you can get away with using lots of inexpensive fabric, such as muslin or poplin, dyed a warm, rich color. Use an expensive fabric or trim for a border or heading, where less yardage is required and it will have maximum impact.

Loose drapes are a way to achieve drama without having to fuss too much. This involves taking a length of fabric and shaping it around your window hardware to create a loosely swagged effect. The fabric should be hemmed and may be lined, but it does not have to be cut into a formal shape. Simply take the length of fabric and drape it around a pole (a decorative pole is best because it will show) installed directly over the window frame. Let the ends hang down gracefully. You can also buy special hardware that will allow you to create a number of decorative effects by draping and knotting the fabric.

Windows that face out on a noisy area or must be protected against extremes of heat or cold should be dressed with heavy, lined draperies. The use of woolens, plaids, or tweeds creates a feeling of coziness.

LININGS

Curtain and drapery linings can seem a daunting topic. Some decorators feel that curtains should always be lined; others, never. Linings serve a number of purposes: they block out light, provide shape to lightweight or medium-weight fabrics, and provide insulation. If a curtain or drape is purely decorative, it probably doesn't need to be lined, unless a lining is required for shape. Or you can have curtains made with detachable linings, so that the lining can be removed for washing or in the summer. Otherwise a traditionally lined or interlined curtain should be dry-cleaned.

Blackout linings are intended to screen out light completely. Such linings are usually made of a special tightly woven fabric with a rubbery feel and a smooth surface. It comes in white or pale colors such as cream or gray, despite the name. Blackout lining is heavy and should not be used to line lightweight fabrics. Instead, you could use tightly woven black cotton as a light-blocking lining. If you are counting on the effect of light shining through to enhance the design of your curtains, blackout lining will obscure it.

Interlining is a heavy, woolly fabric that forms a third layer between the curtain and its backing. It offers extra insulation and helps to change the appearance of the curtain or drapery by softening the folds and making the fabric seem heavier and more opulent. It's one way of getting more mileage out of a cheap fabric, since the soft lining will also make the material seem more luxurious to the touch. Interlined curtains are heavy, so make sure your curtain hardware is well secured to the wall or window frame.

Although linings are traditionally white or a pale color, contrasting linings can be used. If your main curtain fabric is semisheer, a patterned or colored lining will show through and create an interesting effect. With colorful or patterned linings, however, you must also think about how they will look from the outside of the house. Contrasting linings can also be extended out to become borders on the interior side of the window treatment.

TIEBACKS AND TRIMS

Tiebacks and trims are a simple and effective way to add interest to your window treatments. They can also be used to freshen up an existing arrangement if you don't want to throw out your present curtains or drapes. Flat braid or ribbon is a traditional trimming, sewn along the leading edges and bottom of the curtain. Other possibilities are fringe (long or short), fabric piping, ruffles (which can also be piped), and a border of contrasting fabric, which might be padded to add weight and shape.

Materials used as trim might also be used as tiebacks. The tieback can be simply a piece of ribbon or braid or it may be specially sewn. It may match or contrast, be ruffled or piped, padded or shaped. Tiebacks don't even have to be made of fabric. Anything that will go around the curtain and hold it in place will do. Decorating shops and department stores sell ready-made tiebacks and tassels that, depending on your color scheme, can be quite effective. You can also buy decorative metal hooks and rosettes to hold curtains neatly in place.

The placement of the tieback is important. A tight tieback pulls the curtain back straight and creates an angle, while a looser one lets the fabric drape in a deep swag. Tiebacks may be placed high or low.

CHOOSING FABRICS

When shopping for window fabrics, you may find the choice quite bewildering. First, you must decide what you want the window treatment to do. Is it to be purely decorative? Do you need to block strong sunlight or muffle traffic noise from a busy street? Certain fabrics are better suited to a particular use than others. Another consideration is colorfastness. Some types of fabrics, such as silk, tend to fade rapidly when exposed to strong sunlight. Most curtains and drapes will fade eventually, which is why a lining or a separate glass curtain is often employed in traditional window treatments. Other considerations include budget and style. Curtains are expensive. They cost as much as fine clothing (but at least they don't go out of fashion as quickly), and the price of a custom-made set can veer into the haute couture range.

Below is a list of fabric definitions and brief descriptions of how the fabric may best be used.

- *Brocade* A heavy, rich fabric decorated with a raised design of metallic thread, brocade was traditionally made of silk but is now available in cotton and synthetics. It is a very formal fabric and is usually used in period rooms for elaborate draperies.
- *Burlap* A coarse, loosely woven fabric of jute fibers, burlap is humble in origin but can add texture to a room. It's best used for very simple window treatments, such as Roman shades.
- *Canvas* A coarse, heavy, tightly woven fabric, canvas is made from cotton, linen, synthetics, or blends. It is best for use as a simple shade.

- *Damask* Once made of silk and woven in Damascus (hence the name), this fabric can be made of cotton, linen, or wool. The richly figured design is woven into the cloth. It is usually thought of as a fairly formal fabric.
- *Gingham* A cotton fabric, gingham has a striped warp and weft that produces a checked look. The traditional color combinations are red and white or blue and white, but it is seen in many other combinations of colors with white. Usually considered an informal fabric, gingham is appropriate for country-style interiors.
- *Lace* The delicate open work of lace can be made from linen, cotton, silk, metallic, or synthetic threads. Once woven by hand but now mostly machine-made, lace is best used in Victorian or country-style interiors.
- *Muslin* A plain woven cotton, unbleached muslin is a creamy speckled color; bleached muslin is white. It is available in a variety of weights, from heavy and coarse to light and nearly sheer. Since it is relatively inexpensive, it can be used effectively in large quantities for curtains or shades in an informal setting.
- *Organza* Originally made of silk, organza is a stiff and sheer fabric that is now also made from synthetics. It can be used for shades or glass panels.
- *Poplin* A lightweight cotton with a silky finish and a fine ribbed pattern, poplin can be used for a variety of window treatments.
- *Sailcloth* Made of cotton, sailcloth resembles canvas and can be used in the same way.
- *Shirting* Usually made of poplin or fine cotton, shirting is smooth, lustrous, and plainly woven. It is good for fairly informal, unlined curtains.
- *Thai silk* An iridescent, slubbed silk often dyed in bright colors, Thai silk is one of the least expensive and informal silks available.
- *Velvet* Characterized by a short, plushy pile, velvet is woven from cotton or rayon. It is usually used for formal or period rooms.

BLINDS, SHADES, AND SHUTTERS

Shades and blinds, unlike curtains or draperies, simply cover the surface of the window without extending beyond the frame or sill. Shades are generally made of paper, fabric, or plastic. There are two types—roller shades and those controlled by a system of cords, such as Roman or festoon shades. Blinds consist of metal, wood, or plastic slats that are raised or lowered by means of cords.

The plainest shades, when lowered, cover the window with a simple, neat piece of fabric. When raised they take up scarcely any space. Roller shades and Roman shades are among the simplest of fabric shades. Roman shades consist of a panel of fabric lined with horizontal battens that are flat when let down and form a series of crisp pleats when pulled up. They can be lined for insulation and opacity, although blackout or insulated roller shades do the same job. The advantage of roller shades is their crispness and almost architectural simplicity. They are best in streamlined interiors and in rooms with a lot of good decorative detail.

A pleated shade is a modern variation on a Roman shade. Made of stiffened, permanently pleated polyester, they are controlled by cords that run down each side. They are available ready-made in various sizes or can be custom ordered. Another type of pleated shade pulls up from the bottom of the window frame. The main drawback to pleated shades is that, unlike Roman shades, they have no internal frame; the weight of the material pulls down on the pleats and over time they tend to sag. The only solution to this is to replace the shade.

Austrian shades and festoon shades are much more opulent, since they use a good deal of gathered fabric (often referred to as "shirred" or "ruched," which implies that the fabric is gathered tightly into many tiny pleats) and are often trimmed with ruffles or piping. These shades are made from fabric that is twice the width of the window, gathered onto a curtain heading taped to create the shirring, then ruched with cording to form swags. An Austrian shade (sometimes called a balloon shade) is ruched only at the bottom edge, while a festoon shade is ruched all the way up. Both are drawn up by means of cords attached to tiny rings evenly spaced on the back of the shade. They are best made of a relatively plain fabric because the form of the shade itself is so elaborate. They will

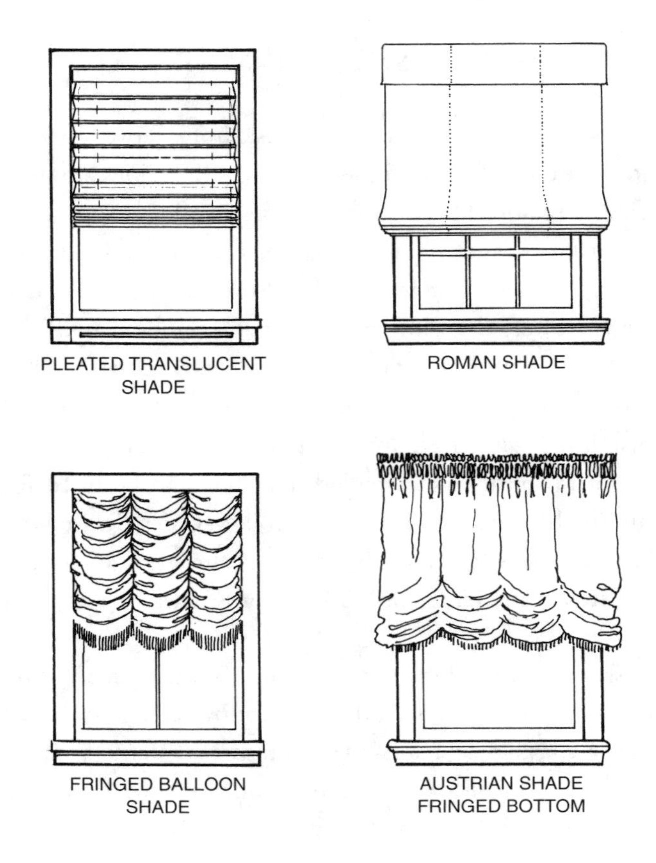

block some of the window even when fully drawn up and therefore should not be used on windows where light is limited.

Matchstick or bamboo blinds (sometimes just called wooden blinds) differ from Venetian blinds in that they are made of split bamboo, matchstick bamboo, or wooden slats woven with string or yarn, and roll up by means of cords that run from top to bottom. They provide privacy yet allow light to filter through. Available in standard sizes, wooden matchstick blinds are best suited to a casual decor.

Venetian blinds, miniblinds, and microblinds are made of slats connected by tapes that are drawn up by means of cords. The slats stack atop one another for a neat look. Venetian blinds are usually made of metal but may also be made of wood, plastic, or stiffened fabric. Miniblinds and microblinds are modern terms describing Venetian blinds with slats only an inch or half an inch deep, with a

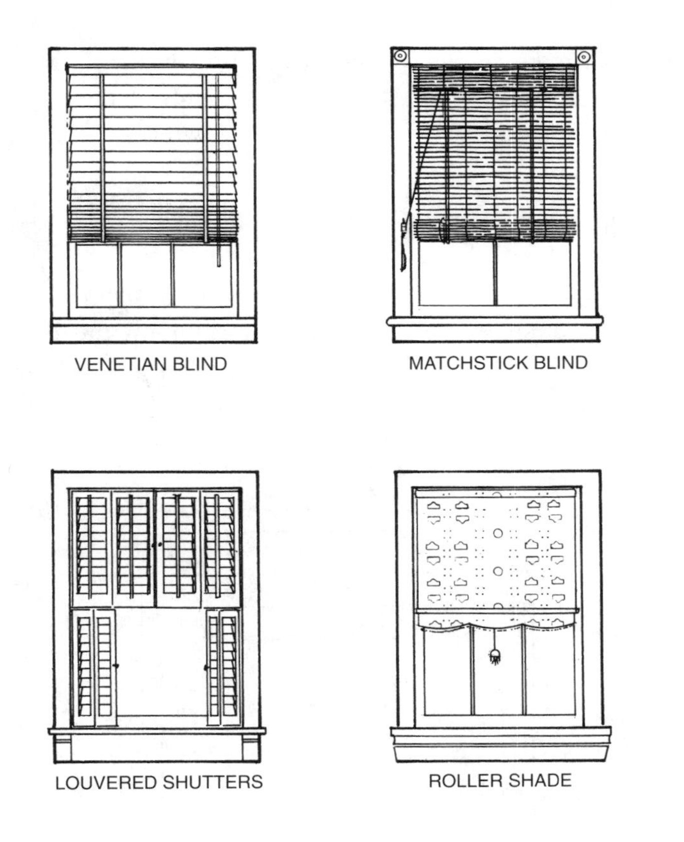

neat, narrow profile. Vertical blinds are like Venetian blinds, but the slats hang vertically. All types of slatted blinds offer a tailored appearance and complete control of light, air, and privacy. They may be used in combination with curtains or draperies for a more formal look.

Louvered and paneled shutters may be stationary or adjustable. Made of wood, they can be used to frame a window or be set inside the window frame in place of curtains. If installed inside the frame, they usually consist of a series of hinged panels with inset louvers that can be adjusted to control light and air. Solid panel indoor shutters are a typical feature of Victorian-era homes and apartments. These may be designed to fit into recesses within the window frame. Some shutters may be fitted with fabric panels rather than louvers for a decorative effect. Shutters can be informal or contemporary in style, depending on the type, and you can add draperies to increase the formality. Unfinished wood shutters, available at lumber and home-center stores, can be painted or stained.

MEASURING WINDOWS AND CALCULATING FABRICS

In order to have curtains or draperies made or make them yourself, you will need to know the dimensions of your windows and how much fabric you will need. Measuring must be done carefully because the effect of many types of window treatments depends on how well they fit the window.

Measuring Windows

WIDTH, DEPENDING ON THE TREATMENT DESIRED:

A. *Measure from one end of the rod to the other, excluding the bent ends (or returns), if any.*

B. *Measure the top of the window frame from one outside edge to the other.*

C. *Measure inside the window frame from one jamb to the other.*

*LENGTH, DEPENDING ON THE TREATMENT DESIRED:**

D. *Measure from the top of the window frame (or rod) to the floor.*

E. *Measure from the top of the window frame (or rod) to the bottom of the sill.*

F. *Measure from the top of the window frame to the top of the sill.*

G. *Measure from the top of the sash to the top of the sill.*

**If you are planning to use rods with rings from which the draperies or curtains will hang, measure from the bottom of the rings.*

To determine the width, measure the length of the rod or pole from which the curtain or drape will hang (see A in illustration). If the rod is a shallow U-shape, be sure to measure the whole thing, not just the front. Then measure the top of the window frame from outside edge to outside edge (B). Measure the inside width of the window from edge to edge (C).

Depending on the type of drapery or curtain you want, you will use one of these measurements to calculate the *width* of the fabric you will need. Generally, for pleated curtains or drapes, the fabric width should be two to three times the width of the window plus the amount needed for hems and overlaps (remember, both sides of each panel will be hemmed, so you must add it four times; overlaps are usually three or more inches deep). For draperies that will extend beyond the window frame, use A as a base; for draperies that will hang to the edge of the frame, use B; and for curtains that will hang within the frame, use C. For shades or blinds that are attached to the window frame, use B; for shades or blinds hung within the frame, use C. If you want curtains that, when drawn, will be completely clear of the window glass, you must add anywhere from six to sixteen inches of fabric on both sides (the rod or pole will have to be this much longer as well).

To determine the *length* of fabric needed, measure from the rod to the floor (D) for floor-length draperies; from the outside top edge of the frame to the outside bottom edge (E) for curtains the same length as the window; from the top edge of the frame to the sill (F) for sill-length curtains; from the inside top edge of the frame to the sill (G) for sill-length curtains that hang inside the window frame. To calculate the fabric needed, add at least three inches for headings and four inches for hems (a total of seven inches). Add an additional two inches for scalloped or tab headings.

To figure out the total yardage you will need, divide the width in inches (A, B, or C plus the amount needed for hems and overlap) by the width of your fabric. Then multiply that figure by the total length (D, E, F, or G plus heading and hem) and divide by thirty-six to get the total number of yards. A calculator helps.

You can also buy simple, ready-made curtain or drapery panels. Check to make sure the finished size will fit your window and hardware. For example, if your curtain rod is thirty-six inches wide, the panel should be at least seventy-two inches wide.

WINDOW HARDWARE

The various types of window rods, poles, clips, and rings may seem bewildering at first, but the great advantage of this profusion is that there's sure to be a type of hardware that is perfectly designed to suit your particular window configurations.

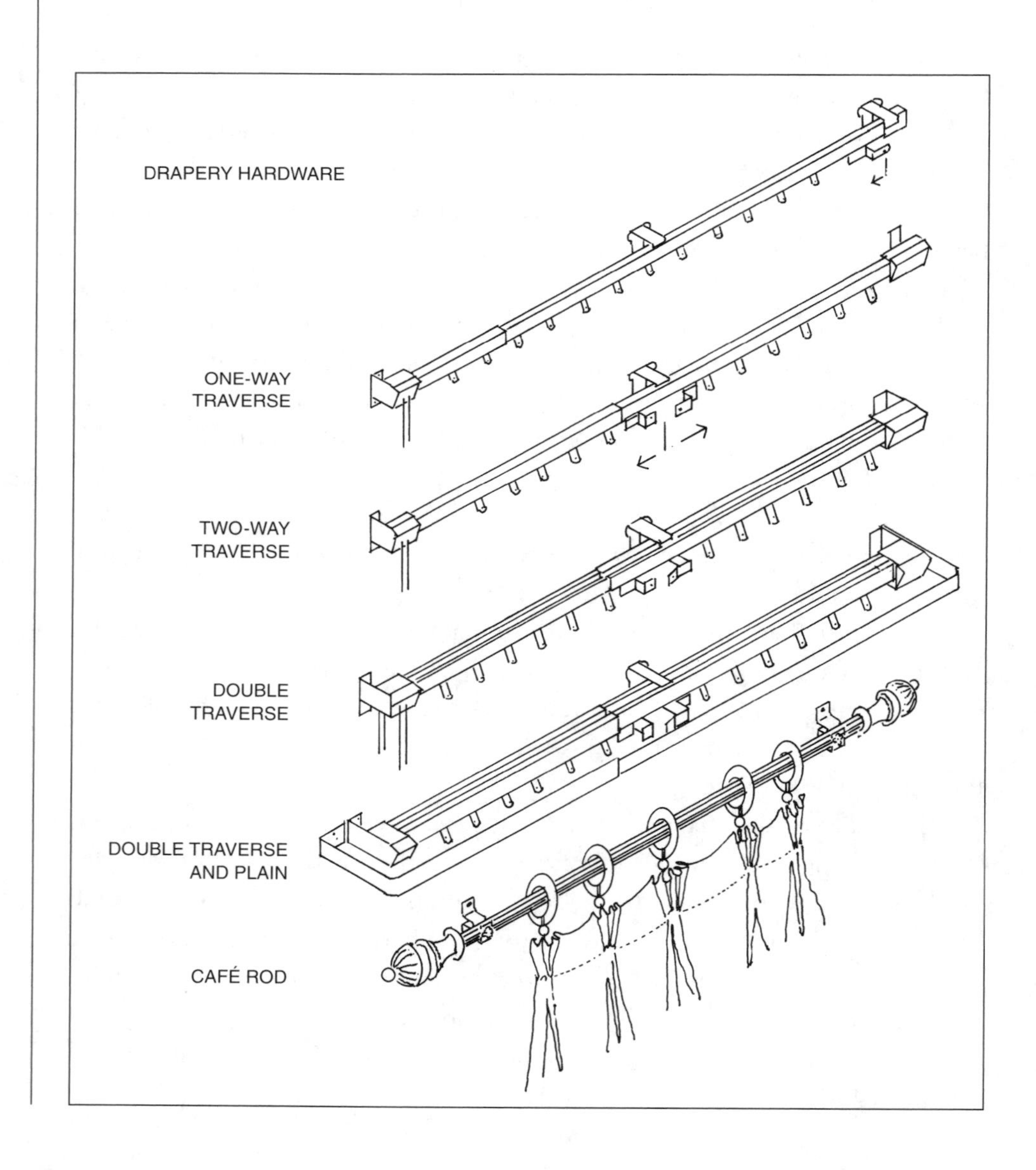

Curtain rods or poles are designed to be used with rod pocket headings, curtains hung from rings, and tab headings. They may be simple tension rods that fit within the window frame or one of various types of rods secured by brackets.

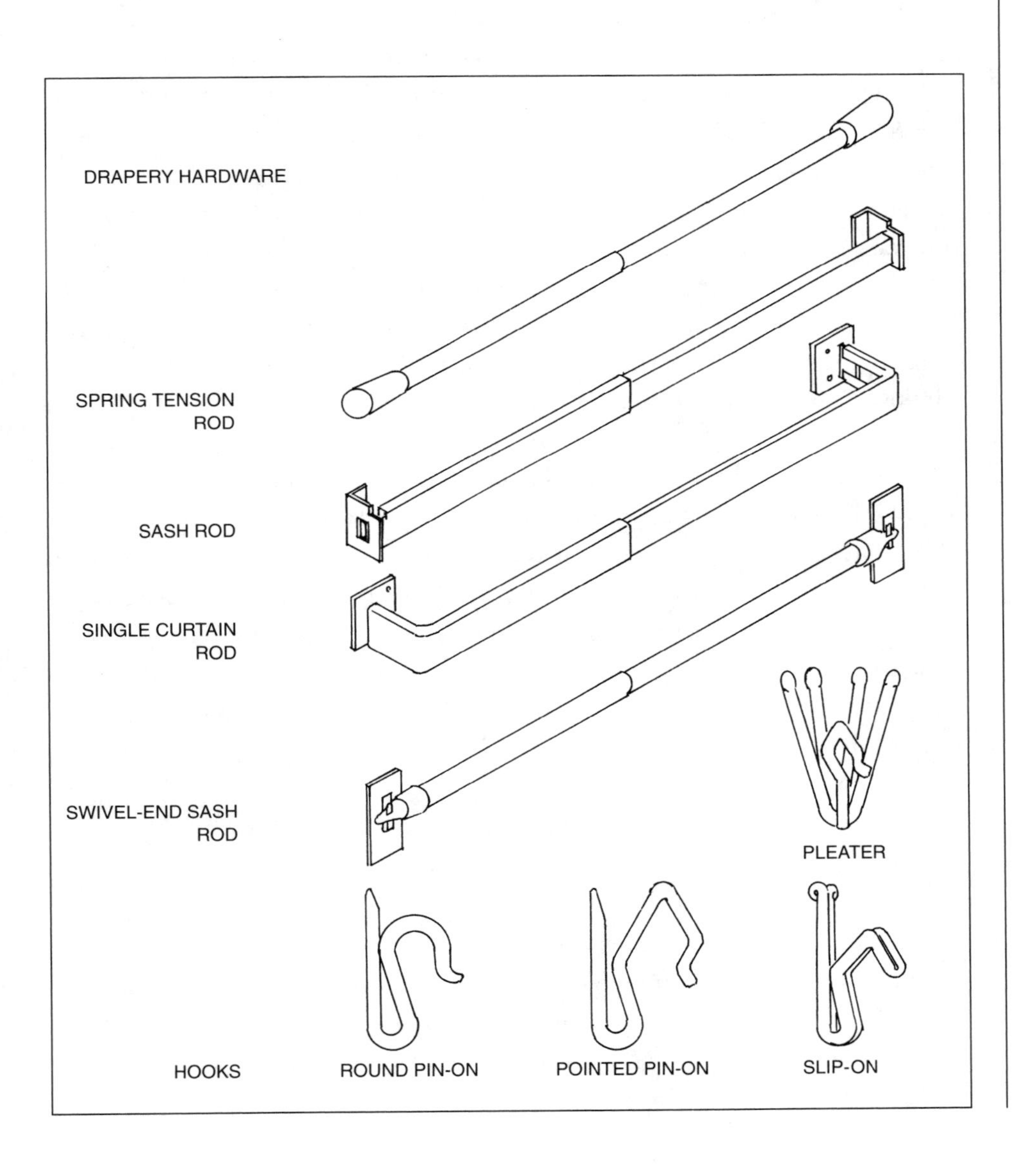

than a rod. Many poles come with decorative finials, which range in shape from a simple ball to an ornate spearhead or fleur-de-lis. Brackets may be adorned in a similar fashion or with flowers or stars. Poles are usually made of metal or wood. The rings that are used to hang the curtain may be decorative in nature and generally are made of the same material as the pole.

Traverse rods are made of plastic or metal, the latter being sturdier. They are fitted with runners that allow the drapery or curtain to glide along the rod. They may come with the draw cords already installed, or the curtains may be drawn by hand. Rods are attached to the wall or window frame by means of brackets, usually one at each end and one or more in between, depending on the length of the rod. Double rods or special extension brackets are available if you want to hang more than one set of curtains or drapes. The curtain heading should conceal a traverse rod completely when closed; often a decorative heading such as a cornice or valance is installed to conceal the rod completely. Traverse rods are versatile, as they can be bent to follow the curve of bay or bow windows. There is also a type designed to be bent to the curve of a Palladian window.

With the exception of rod pocket curtains, which simply slip over the rod or pole, hooks are used to attach the curtain or drapery to the rod or pole. These slide into special pockets of the heading tape (see page 194) and then attach to the runners of a traverse rod or the rings of a pole. Rings may also be clipped or sewn to the curtain heading. Hooks usually have a single prong, but pleater hooks, used with goblet or cartridge pleat headings, have several. Pin-on hooks, which have sharp points, are used with hand-sewn headings. Hooks may also be sewn on by hand.

EXERCISES

1. List facts about each window—measurements and requirements (the need to block light or noise, hide an ugly view, give privacy, and so on). Annotate the room plan or devote a page in your notebook for each window or set of windows in a particular room.

2. Think about what kind of effect you want to create. Should the window be simple and informal? Simple but elegant? Would your overall decor be best suited by a complex window treatment or a less elaborate one?

3. Make a separate list of problem windows, including windows that contain air-conditioning units, are an unusual size or shape, or are in an awkward spot. Note if you will have to deal with the problem by purchasing special or custom-made hardware. A good snapshot or two will help you in describing your problem to salespeople.

4. Study decorating magazines carefully, since they often feature information on window treatments. Clip pages or make note of designs that appeal to you, and think about how you might re-create them in your own home.

Decorating your windows may seem a daunting prospect, but if you keep the basic facts in mind you should keep your sanity. First, think about what problem you need to solve—to create privacy, to block light, or to camouflage an unattractive view (or frame a gorgeous one). Once you've come up with a solution to this problem, think of a way to make it fit with your room scheme. Finally, keep it simple. Unless your home is decorated in an elaborate period style and is extremely formal, you probably do not need to create complicated window treatments.

16

✦ ✦

LIGHTING

In the home, lighting must serve two purposes. It must be decorative (the type of fixture or lamp you choose must fit into the overall scheme of a room) and practical (it must shed sufficient light for the space it is illuminating). In addition, light itself can be used as a decorating tool, enhancing other aspects of a room's decoration, picking out architectural details, emphasizing texture and proportion, or spotlighting a treasured vase or painting. The right kind of lighting can even make a small room seem larger.

Different people have different priorities. Some prefer light fixtures to be entirely practical and almost invisible, while others love ornate lamps and ruffled shades. The choice, of course, is yours.

LIGHTING PRINCIPLES

Ambient or *general lighting,* as the term suggests, provides an overall level of light and helps to make you aware of the proportion and size of a room or area. It serves as a nighttime substitute for daylight. It can be supplied by a number of different types of fixtures, including ceiling-mounted lights, wall lights, uplights, and table lamps.

CHECKLIST

1. Do you have a floor plan of the room with outlets indicated?
2. Is there a sufficient number of outlets? If not, you will need to add more or install built-in lighting.
3. Have you thought about where you need to add light?
4. Have you made a list of areas that require special lighting?
5. Will you need to hire an electrician?
6. Have you considered reusing or adapting your present light fixtures?
8. Have you considered installing dimmer switches?

Lighting Mounting Heights

One aim of good lighting placement is that the bare light bulb is never seen.

A. *A sconce should be above eye level when standing (more than 65 inches).*★

B. *A table or standing reading lamp should be at or slightly below eye level when seated (more than 44 inches).*

C. *A hanging light over a dining table should be just above one's head when seated (from 54 to 58 inches).*

★The new A.D.A. law does not permit a projection greater than 4 inches from a wall when that object is 27 inches to 80 inches above the floor.

Task lighting is the light you work by. You need to install task lighting anywhere you perform an activity (cooking, sewing, reading, playing games) and need to be able to see things clearly and comfortably. Position a task light so that shadows do not fall across your work. Adjustable lamps that can be angled to suit the requirements of the task at hand, such as downlights, angled desk lamps, and spotlights, are often the best choice.

Utility lighting is functional rather than decorative. It is the type of lighting used to illuminate potentially dangerous areas, such as steep basement stairways, the steps up to the front porch, or the area just outside the entry to an apartment.

Accent lighting is decorative and dramatic. Use it to emphasize special objects or decorative features. It can be built in or come from a special small fixture. Directional spotlights that cast a single strong beam of light are useful for this purpose; other suitable types include traditional picture lights, concealed undershelf lighting, and uplights.

The three main types of light sources used in residences include tungsten, halogen, and fluorescent. Tungsten light comes from traditional light bulbs, which cast a warm, yellowish light. Their advantage is that they are widely available and inexpensive; their disadvantages include the need for frequent replacement, excessive heat generation, and inefficient energy use.

Halogen light sources cast a cool and crisp light that is whiter and brighter than that from standard tungsten bulbs. They have a "sparkling" quality that works well in accent fixtures. They are expensive, however, and some types must be used with a transformer, which adds to the cost of the fixture. In addition, they generate a lot of heat and must be used with a filter (most bulbs come with their own built-in filter) to prevent exposure to harmful UV rays.

Fluorescent bulbs and tubes use the least amount of energy, but many types emit a light that alters the appearance of colors, making them look dull. Full-spectrum fluorescent tubes most closely resemble true sunlight. All fluorescent lamps require a special adapter if you want to use them with a dimmer.

Lighting your home consumes energy, so in addition to making sure everything is well lit, you should ensure that your lighting system is energy efficient. One way of doing this is to buy compact fluorescent bulbs. One 18-watt compact fluorescent bulb gives the same amount of light as a 75-watt incandescent lamp and lasts an astonishing thirteen times longer (that means that for every compact fluorescent bulb you buy, you would have had to buy more than three of those four-bulb packs). In addition, use of these bulbs saves energy and reduces pollution.

Another way to save energy is to light the walls rather than the floor. Walls are what most people look at rather than the floor, and lighting the walls will make the room seem larger. This means eliminating central ceiling fixtures as much as possible. Another powerful tool in a lighting scheme is a dimmer, because you can control the level of light as you wish. The number of fixtures required depends not only on the size of the room but on the types of fixtures used. Here are some guidelines adapted from those put out by the American Lighting Association:

Area	*Pendants and Ceiling Lights*	*Recessed Fixtures*	*Wall Lights*
Room under 150 square feet	Three to five incandescent lamps for a total of 100 to 150 watts (35 to 60 fluorescent watts)	Four 75-watt incandescent lamps (80 fluorescent watts)	Four 50-watt reflector bulbs (60 to 80 fluorescent watts)
Room 150 to 250 square feet	Four to six incandescent lamps for a total of 200 to 300 watts (60 to 80 fluorescent watts)	Four 100-watt incandescent lamps (120 fluorescent watts)	Five to eight 75-watt incandescent reflector lamps (120 to 160 fluorescent watts)
Room over 250 square feet	One incandescent lamp per 125 square feet for a total of 1 watt (1/3 fluorescent watt) per square foot	100 to 150 incandescent watts for every 50 square feet (160 to 200 fluorescent watts)	One 75-watt incandescent reflector lamp per 25 square feet (160 fluorescent watts)

For more information, contact the American Lighting Association at 1-800-BRIGHT-IDEAS.

CEILING LIGHTS, SPOTLIGHTS, AND WALL LIGHTS

Ceiling and pendant fixtures are a traditional way of lighting a room and adding dramatic and decorative flare. However, don't count on a single central fixture for all of your lighting needs, even in a small room. First of all, a fixture like this lights mainly the floor, which is not what you want people to look at. Second, it doesn't give enough illumination, even when fitted with a couple of 100-watt bulbs. Distribute that wattage around the room and you'll find that you get much better results.

Ceiling pendant lamps are most useful over dining tables or library tables (although you might want to add a specific task light as well if people will be using the table for studying) as well as coffee tables, where they serve to provide ambient light for conversation and entertaining. A bulb with a silvered crown, which reduces glare, is best in these types of fixtures. Pendant fixtures should be fifty-eight to sixty-three inches from the floor.

A chandelier is a special type of ceiling fixture that provides several small light sources, sometimes emphasized with reflectors or prisms. Chandeliers are highly dramatic but useful only as ambient light. The amount of light they cast depends on the overall wattage they contain.

The amount of light you will get from a ceiling fixture depends on how it is shaded and what type of bulb you use. Translucent glass and ceramic shades allow light to diffuse evenly in all directions, while reflectors and opaque shades direct light in one direction, usually down. Spotlights create concentrated beams, while floodlights give a wider, cone-shaped area of light and standard light bulbs provide diffuse, overall illumination.

Downlights are high-tech fixtures recessed into or mounted on the ceiling to cast pools of light on whatever is below them. They may be fitted with spotlights, floods, or ordinary light bulbs, depending on the type of illumination desired. They can also be mounted with swivels so that you can adjust them to direct light at a wall or other surface. They are especially useful for illuminating work surfaces such as kitchen counters or desktops.

Spotlights also can be either recessed or surface mounted. They are available as ceiling-mounted clusters that can be pointed in a variety of directions or as clusters mounted on a pole (often called a pole lamp). They are also available as individual lights on clips or clamps, which can be attached to a shelf or molding and relocated as needed. Depending on the type of bulb used, spotlights can provide general background illumination or be trained on a specific spot as accent lighting. You might want to use a silvered-crown bulb to prevent glare if the shade (sometimes called a shutter) leaves the face of the bulb visible.

Wall lights may serve a similar purpose. These come in various styles, from traditional bracket lights to ultramodern metal or plaster sconces, and are usually used in pairs. In general, wall lights should be used to provide ambient lighting.

TABLE AND FLOOR LAMPS

Table and floor lamps are the mainstay of most domestic lighting schemes. They can provide both task lighting and ambient lighting. As decorative objects they can be purchased in a wide range of styles.

Depending on the style of your room, certain types of floor and table lamps will be more appropriate than others. The following will give you an idea of which types of shades and bases suit which interiors.

Table lamps, depending on the type of shade, will either shed light up and down or spread it horizontally. Translucent fabric shades diffuse light best for general ambiance, followed by linen, cardboard, and paper. Shades should be deep enough to shield your eyes from the light source, whether you are sitting or standing. Several table lamps used around a room will create an atmospheric look, with pools of light surrounded by shadow. Some of this light is directed up to the ceiling, thus increasing the general light level as well. There should be thirty-nine to forty inches between the bottom of the shade and the floor for the best overall effect.

Directional lamps, reading lamps, or work lights should be adjustable to shed light where it is needed. The classic modern design for a desk lamp is known as an anglepoise or architect's lamp, with a deep cowl shade and a metal stand that bends and swivels to cast light wherever needed. They clamp onto your work surface or stand on a weighted base. Traditional brass "reading lamps" with green glass shades are another option. For a desk lamp, the light source should be fifteen inches above the work surface.

Floor lamps, like table lamps, can be used to supply ambient light or task lighting. Standard lamps, also known as bridge lamps, look best in period rooms; halogen or incandescent standing uplights (also called torchieres) are more modern in appearance. Some have adjustable shades. A standard floor lamp should measure forty-two to forty-nine inches from the bottom of the shade to the floor.

Style	*Base*	*Shade*
Country	Reproduction oil lamps in tole, pewter, or brass; ceramic jugs, crocks, or jars; metal canisters	White or pale silk or parchment shade; enamel or marbleized paper
Formal	Candlestick, column, ginger jar, cylinder, or vase forms in porcelain or glass	Patterned or solid fabric or paper, metal or glass
Modern	Chrome, glass, or matte-black metal; colored plastic	Metal; opaque, clear, or sandblasted glass or plastic

Uplights are downlights in reverse and usually sit on the floor. They are easy to install because they can be plugged into a wall outlet and concealed behind furniture or in corners to create dramatic accent lighting.

TRACK LIGHTING

Originally designed for industrial and commercial use, track lighting provides a number of light sources but requires only a single power source. It is wonderful if you need to install additional lighting and can't afford to have a lot of expensive electrical work done. The track mounts to the ceiling or wall and can be fitted with downlights and spots to provide lighting where needed. It is best if used directionally, to bounce light off the ceiling or floor or to spotlight a piece of art.

The tracks that hold the actual fixtures come in two types, open and closed. Open tracks have the advantage of allowing you to move lights around on the track, but they also accumulate dust and grease, especially when used in the kitchen, and can be difficult to clean. Closed tracks, which feature a cover that hooks on, don't have this problem but lack the flexibility of open-track systems.

WIRING

Be careful not to overload outlets, which can cause a fire. If you need to install additional wiring but can't or don't want to run it under the floor or through the wall or ceiling, you can install a covered conduit mounted on the surface of the wall. It provides a raised channel to contain the necessary wires and has a snap-on cover to conceal them. A conduit is least obtrusive when run either at floor level or at ceiling height. As with other electrical work, this type of channel should be installed by a licensed electrician.

Lamp and fixture cords can serve as a decorative as well as a functional element. They can be colored, twisted, or coiled to provide visual interest, especially in a modern room or a child's room.

EXERCISES

Proper lighting makes any decorating scheme look better, but many people find lighting "too technical" and feel daunted at the prospect of creating a pleasing and functional lighting scheme. However, if you approach the task with plenty of common sense and allow adequate time, you should have no trouble. Sit in the room under various lighting conditions (both during the day and at night) and think about where the light falls. Note problems (such as insufficiently lighted areas) on a sheet of paper or a copy of the room plan. Then go ahead and complete the following exercises and you will be well on your way to developing a successful and attractive lighting scheme.

1. For each room that you are decorating, make a list of the activities that require illumination. You might include, for example, reading, sewing or knitting, watching television or videotapes, cooking and food preparation, dining, and so on.

2. On a floor plan, mark the areas where these activities take place and note what kind of lighting exists there now and what needs to be added.

3. What type of natural light does the room receive? Natural lighting is the most pleasing to the eye. Your lighting scheme will be most successful if you use the way the daylight falls in the room as a guide. Try to develop a lighting scheme that echoes the fall of natural light (that is, it should come from the direction of the windows or from above).

17

WALLS AND WOODWORK

Walls play an important visual role in decoration because, along with floors, they form the most extensive surface area of your home. The two most common types of wall treatments are wallpaper and paint. Wallpaper is flexible, is available in a wide range of colors, textures, and patterns, is relatively easy to install, and helps brighten up any room. Most types are easy to keep clean and last for several years.

Paint provides the cheapest and quickest method of changing the appearance of a room. It comes in an infinite variety of colors and can be applied by sponging, ragging, and stenciling to create various effects. Paint can be used to enhance a room with simple effects, such as accenting the molding in a color different from the walls or glazing a base color with thin coats of wash in a slightly different color to create luminosity and depth.

Instead of painting or wallpapering, you may want to tile a wall, cover it with fabric, or panel it. These approaches cost more than painting or papering and require a certain skill to install; in fact, tiling should be done by a professional. Fabrics and wood paneling cost more than wallpaper but are useful if you need to disguise a particularly lumpy or discolored wall or you want to create a special effect.

MEASURING WALLS

Regardless of the type of wall treatment you have chosen, you must start by estimating the area that is going to be covered. This is simple to do. First, measure around the perimeter of the room, including all of the alcoves and jogs in the wall, then multiply by the ceiling height. This will give you the total wall area.

PAINTING

The two types of paint used in most interior applications are latex (water-based) and oil based. Latex paint dries quickly and can be cleaned up with water. Oil-based paint takes longer to dry than latex and must be removed in cleanup with

CHECKLIST

1. Have you measured the walls completely, including the ceiling area? (See "Measuring Walls," next page.)
2. Have you tested your paint color by hanging up a large sample or by painting a section of the wall to make sure it really pleases you?
3. Have you made sure that your paint, fabric, or wall-covering samples really do match or harmonize with the other colors in your decor?
4. Have you double-checked your estimate of the amount of wallpaper or paint you need?
5. If you are doing the job yourself, are you sure you have all the equipment you need to do it properly?
6. Have you set aside enough time for your project?

a solvent such as turpentine; also, it must be applied over an oil-based undercoat. Both types of paint are available in a range of finishes, from high gloss to flat, and in a variety of colors. Enamel paint is a type of oil-based paint that is very dense and has an extremely high gloss. It is usually applied only on small areas of wood or metal.

If you can't find the perfect color or if you want to match a particular color or create a series of harmonious tints, you can mix your own colors using artist's oil or acrylic pigments. If using oils, mix the pigment with turpentine and add it to a white base (special paints are sold for this purpose, but you can also use regular oil-based paint). With acrylics use water as a solvent to dissolve the pigment and then combine it with a white latex base.

Depending on the surface you are painting, a quart of undercoat will cover from 120 to 150 square feet. A quart of latex paint will cover 130 to 140 square feet, depending on the finish (semigloss and matte-finish paints go a bit farther), and a quart of oil-based paint covers 160 to 170 square feet (the glossier finish covers a slightly greater area).

Before you paint, clear the room of furniture as much as possible. Remove lamp shades and take down curtains. Cover the remaining furniture and the floor with dust sheets and drop cloths. Walls and ceilings in good condition need to be vacuumed or dusted, then washed with a solution of detergent and water before painting. Cracks and holes in the walls should be patched and filled and the patches primed before painting. Peeling paint should be scraped and the wall surface washed. Wallpaper should be removed before a wall is painted.

Paint the room surfaces in this order: the ceiling, working away from the natural light source; walls; and window frames and doors. Finish up with moldings and picture railings. Baseboards should come last. If you use a wide brush, roller, or pad, apply the paint in random directions rather than just up and down or back and forth. Work out from corners, which should be cut in with a smaller brush. Overlap and criss-cross your strokes. When you finish painting a section or need to get more paint, end with a light, upward stroke to eliminate marks.

Paint Effects

Following is a brief overview of techniques you can use to create special surface effects with paint. Detailed how-to pamphlets from large paint manufacturers can often be found where paints are sold.

- *Dragging or Strié* This technique creates a subtle, variegated surface and requires the application of a thick transparent glaze over a base color. You then use a wide, dry brush to "drag" the wet surface and remove paint so that the base color shows through. Stippling is the opposite of dragging; you use a brush loaded with glaze to apply transparent color over the wall in an irregular fashion. You can use wads of crumpled stiff paper rather than a brush for a similar effect.
- *Sponging* In a way, sponging is similar to stippling because color is applied to the wall rather than removed from it. The tool of choice here is a large sponge, which produces an irregular, splotchy effect.
- *Stenciling* You can either use a stencil kit or make your own stencils by tracing a design onto a sheet of stiff paper, acetate, or Mylar, then cutting it out with an X-Acto knife. It's best to use fairly thick

paint (thin paint may run under the edge of your stencil and ruin the image) and a small sponge or stiff-bristle stencil brush so that you can control the application of paint.

- *Rag Rolling* Also known as ragging, this method produces a blurry, cloudlike layer of color. You use bunched rags or wads of paper or plastic to apply paint to the wall.

WALLPAPER

Wall coverings are available in a wide range of patterns and materials, from paper to vinyl. Some coverings are designed with matching borders and coordinating patterns that can be used to decorate rooms that lead into one another. Others are designed to mimic paint effects or other materials, such as fabric or woodgrain. Some are actually paper-backed natural fibers, such as burlap and grasscloth, which are usually expensive but provide a textured, neutral-tone background that adds interest to a room.

Wallpaper varies in quality. Less expensive papers tend to be thinner, making them difficult to hang. More costly coverings pay off by being easier for the amateur to put up. The most expensive papers are hand-printed designs, often reproductions of antiques, sometimes made from the original printing blocks.

Most types of wallpapers are treated to repel moisture. "Spongeable" papers are covered with a plastic film and can be washed with water; "scrubbable" papers have a thick vinyl coating and can actually be scrubbed. They are best for use in kitchens, bathrooms, and laundry rooms—wherever there is a high moisture content in the air.

Once you have measured your total wall area, you will need to estimate how many rolls of wall covering to buy. In order to estimate the number of rolls you need, divide the total wall area of the room by the number of square feet in a roll. One roll of American wallpaper covers thirty square feet; a roll of European wallpaper covers twenty-three square feet. To make your estimate more precise, subtract one-half roll for each window or door. Round up to the nearest whole roll. If your paper has a repeating pattern that must be matched, add an extra one to three rolls to make sure you don't come up short.

The best order for papering a room is to start in the corner nearest the window and work away from the source of natural light toward the door. That way any slight overlaps will be less likely to cast shadows and will call less attention to themselves. Always apply wallpaper to a clean, even, dry surface. If there are a lot of cracks and irregularities, you will need to patch the wall first or put up lining paper. Hanging wallpaper requires the following tools and equipment:

- Wallpaper paste, unless paper is prepasted
- Pasting table or board over sawhorses
- Plumb line (to find the true vertical)
- Pencil and ruler
- Stepladder
- Shears or scissors
- Paste brush, bucket, paper brush, water, and sponge

See the Bibliography for any of the decorating books by Mary Gilliatt, which contain chapters on decorating with wallpaper, including complete instructions on hanging wallpaper.

TILING

Tiled walls are rare in most American homes, except in kitchens and baths. Some of the types you may want to consider are ceramic tiles, which can range from the familiar mass-produced square tiles used in baths and showers to expensive hand-made, hand-painted tile murals; mirror tiles, which are inexpensive, easy to install, and can make a small area seem much larger; and other types of tile, such as cork.

Mosaic tiles are a special category. Available in beautiful, rich colors, they may be made of marble, clay, or glass with a high silica content. Because they are small (one inch square or smaller), they come mounted on a peel-off backing, making them easier to lay. Mosaic tiles are difficult to obtain through standard retail outlets; you may have to order them through a tile specialist or showroom.

FABRIC WALLS

The two most common methods of decorating walls with fabric are shirring and stapling. Covering walls with gathered fabric—shirring—creates a soft, romantic effect. Fabric is gathered at the top and bottom edges, then fixed to the walls in one of several ways. The edges may be gathered on dowels installed at cornice and baseboard level. Or the fabric may be attached to the wall with heavy-duty Velcro tapes or mounted on a special track system (generally available only through professional designers or decorators). For the dowel method the fabric is hemmed so that the dowels can be slipped through. Since each wall requires about three times its width in fabric, it's best to limit shirring to small rooms or use relatively inexpensive fabric, such as muslin, voile, or sheeting. You can also hang fabric against the wall like a curtain, which can then be drawn back to expose doorways, built-in shelving, and the like.

Fabric with a fairly tight, flat weave can be attached to walls using a staple gun. Cut the fabric into panels the size and shape of your walls (you will need to seam it or glue it to make large panels) and then staple it along the cornice or ceiling line, smoothing (not stretching) it as you go along. Then conceal the staples with trim. If you don't want to staple fabric directly to the wall, use wooden battens installed at cornice and baseboard levels around the room.

WOODWORK

If you live in an older building that has been stripped of its traditional woodwork, adding new trim and details will help restore the original look. Many types of wood trim are available from the lumberyard, and there are specialty lumberyards that carry an even broader range of trim and woodwork if you can't find what you want in your area. Trim and details made of wood can be expensive, but there are many catalogs and home-decorating stores that offer decorative details such as ceiling rosettes or cornice moldings in skillfully cast resin. These can be painted like wood and, if well made, bear a striking resemblance to authentic examples of such details.

Wood paneling is another decorative possibility. Tongue-and-groove paneling, the most commonly available, is mounted on the existing wall using wood battens known as furring strips. Paneling has a very traditional, warm, rich appearance but can be very expensive. You can achieve a somewhat similar effect for less money by installing a paneled dado (wainscot) to waist height or halfway up the wall. All paneling, whether new or old, can be varnished, stained, or painted.

EXERCISES

Remember, walls take up a good portion of the surface area of your home, so it's worth your while to put time and energy into dealing with them, whatever treatment you choose. One of the most important things about walls, even before deciding on a decorative technique, is making certain that they are in tiptop condition. A lumpy wall, or one webbed with fine cracks, is never going to look the way you want it to with some type of remedial treatment. You'll be surprised, though, at what you can achieve with walls in less-than-perfect condition.

1. Carefully inspect your existing walls. Check their condition and make a list of those that need repair or a different type of treatment to camouflage the defects. List these areas and decide how best to cope with the problem. For example, you may need to put up a washable wallpaper or use easy-to-clean high-gloss paint.

____

____

____

____

____

Meinl

18

FLOORS

Whatever flooring material you choose must be hard-wearing, since floors take more of a beating than any other surface in the home. Floors also cover a lot of space, so new flooring materials inevitably will be a large item in your redecorating budget. The most practical and economical approach is to think of your floors as a neutral background. Even with cost restraints you have plenty of choices, from vinyl tile to wall-to-wall carpeting. Some people prefer wood floors, which are available in a number of styles and prices. You may find that information on flooring refers to "hard" and "soft" types; hard refers to wood, tile, or vinyl, while soft comprises all forms of carpeting and rugs.

HARDWOOD AND PARQUET

Natural wood flooring adds warmth to a room and feels comfortable underfoot. It may be made of hardwood, such as white or red oak (perhaps the most popular), walnut, cherry, birch, poplar, or maple; the last three are much paler than the others and also much softer. Flooring may also be made of softwood, such as pine, larch, spruce, cedar, redwood, hemlock, or fir. The boards may be of any width, with two-and-a-half-inch-wide strip flooring of oak being the most common type.

CHECKLIST

1. In choosing a flooring, have you considered durability and the amount of traffic the area will receive?
2. Have you thought about whether your existing floors can be repaired or renovated?
3. Have you chosen a final color scheme for the room?
4. Have you checked to make sure your samples of paint, wall covering, and upholstery really do match or harmonize with your flooring materials?

Depending on the type of heating system you have, moisture content in the air may affect your choice of wood. With standard central heating the moisture content should be 10 to 14 percent; with under-floor heating it should be about half that. Ask your supplier how moisture content will affect your choice of flooring.

Decorative parquet floors are associated with the Victorian era. These floors are made of different types of wood, sometimes combining light and dark, joined together in herringbone, checkered, or striped patterns. They are also available as twelve-inch squares in more complex patterns, such as basket weave. Using wood tiles you can even design your own parquet floor, perhaps combining a checkerboard with a striped or patterned border.

All types of wooden flooring should be sealed with either a penetrating oil sealer (with wax for protection) or a waterproof polyurethane. Most types of manufactured floors are presealed.

NATURAL TILE

Natural tile, whether ceramic or stone, comes in many different forms, almost all of them hard-wearing and impervious to water, mud, and grease. All types of natural tile connote luxury (because of its high cost compared to other types of flooring) and permanence, so you may want to restrict its use to small areas, such as entryways. While stone tile (granite, marble, or slate) is often the most expensive, highly decorative ceramic tile, especially if it is hand-painted, can be quite pricey too. Tile has the possible disadvantages of being cold underfoot (which actually can be an advantage in warm climates) and noisy under hard-soled shoes because the tile itself is very hard. Things dropped on it are more likely to break, and in the bathroom, it can be slippery (see Chapter 11, "The Bathroom"). One final point: tile is heavy, so make sure that the subflooring in the area where you plan to install it is strong enough to bear its weight.

Ceramic tile is made from baked and glazed clay and is available in a broad range of sizes, textures, and colors. *Quarry* tile is made from unrefined clay with a high quartz content. It comes in square, rectangular, or hexagonal shapes in warm, natural tones. *Brick* tile (also called a paver) is too heavy to install above the ground floor. It comes in a variety of colors, from the standard red-brown to the more unusual green, blue, and purple. It does not need to be sealed and is easy to care for.

Since it tends to be expensive and difficult to handle, the most practical way to use *marble* in the home is in tile form. *Slate* tile, like brick, should be used only on the ground floor of a house. Although beautiful and durable, slate is expensive and difficult to install. *Stone* flooring is unusual and beautiful too. Many types of natural stone can be used for flooring, including granite, sandstone, and limestone, although some types absorb stains easily. *Terrazzo* tile is made of chips of granite or stone embedded in a composite base. It is quite elegant and is available in many colors. Terrazzo wears well and is relatively easy to install, but it can be expensive.

Mosaic tiles may be made of marble, clay, or glass with a high silica content and come in beautiful, rich colors. They come mounted on a peel-off backing, which makes them easier to lay. *Cork* tile, made of pressed and baked cork, is warm and comfortable underfoot. It is softer than other types of tile and must be sealed for durability.

VINYL

Vinyl flooring is easy to install because it can be put down over almost any other type of flooring and requires very little preparation. Vinyl sheeting is available in six-, nine-, and twelve-foot-wide rolls, which reduces the need for seams. Some sheet vinyl has a foam backing, making it softer and easier on the feet than any other type of flooring except carpet. Sheet flooring is easiest to lay down in large spaces, while vinyl tiles are easier to install in smaller, more irregularly shaped rooms. Tiles are available in patterns that imitate ceramic or natural stone tile and come in various sizes, although twelve inches square is the most common. Some come with an adhesive backing and can simply be pressed into place. Whether in sheet or tile form, vinyl is relatively inexpensive, durable, easy to keep clean, waterproof, and stain resistant. Other types of synthetic hard-surface flooring include asbestos and rubber tile. Asbestos costs less than vinyl but tends to show wear and soil more easily. Rubber, although handsome and springy underfoot, needs waxing to keep its color and costs more than vinyl.

CARPET

Wall-to-wall carpeting can be a good flooring choice for many rooms. It is warm and soft underfoot, fairly easy to keep clean, and relatively inexpensive compared to other types of flooring. It is available in many styles and in a range of prices. Heavy, dense carpets with a short pile are the most durable.

Carpeting is made of different types of fibers and backings. In a woven carpet, the pile and backing are woven together, while in a tufted carpet the fibers are inserted into a separate backing, then sealed with adhesive. Woven carpets should be installed over underlayment (carpet padding).

The following are some of the carpet terms you may encounter:

- *Axminster* is a woven carpet with a tufted pile. The pile may be of any height. This type of construction is used for patterned carpets.
- *Berber* is a fleecy carpet with a low, nubby pile, often tweedy in effect.
- *Broadloom* is a standard term describing carpet produced in widths over six feet (twelve and fifteen feet are the most common).
- *High-and-low-looped carpet* has a sculptured surface and is very durable.
- *Plush velvet carpet* has an evenly cut, dense pile that is durable but shows traffic wear and footprints.
- *Random-sheared carpet* has a pile with some high-sheared strands and low loops, giving it a sculptured effect. It wears well but may flatten in high-traffic areas.
- *Shag carpeting* has long yarns, either sheared or looped, from three-quarters to two inches long. It may mat in high-traffic areas.
- *Tip-sheared carpet* mixes loops with cut pile, all the same length to reduce wear.

- *Twist carpet* has a looped surface of twisted yarns. It does not readily show wear.

The fibers used in carpets include wool, nylon, polyester, polypropylene (olefin), and acrylic. They may be used alone or in blends. Although expensive, wool carpeting is luxurious and durable, with excellent resistance to wear. It holds colors well and is available in a wide selection of styles. Nylon, sold under the trade names Antron, Anso, Enkalon, Ultron, and Zeftron, is soft, wears well, and is less expensive than wool. It can be treated with a stain-resistant coating that makes it very easy to keep clean. Polyester fiber does not wear as well as wool or nylon and has poor resistance to oil-based stains. It is soft to the touch and costs less than wool or nylon. Brand names are Dacron, Fortrel, and Trevira. Polypropylene is not quite as resilient as the previously mentioned fibers but has excellent stain resistance and is relatively inexpensive. Available in limited colors, it is often used for indoor-outdoor carpeting. Brand names are Herculon, Marvess, Marquesa-Lana, and Vectra. Acrylic fiber is used not for broadloom carpeting but in area rugs and may be cut to fit bathrooms and other small areas. Not as resilient or wear- and stain-resistant as wool or nylon, it is very soft and comes in a wide variety of colors.

Matting of coir, sisal grass, or rush (all different types of plant fibers) is a neutral alternative to carpet. If you don't have or can't afford wood flooring, matting makes a good replacement. While matting is not as soft underfoot as carpeting, it does offer textural contrast and a variety of patterns, including basket weave, herringbone, and stripes. It also comes in colors, mainly earth tones, and may be stenciled or painted.

AREA RUGS

If you have a hard floor that you want to soften or liven up, area rugs are the best choice. To avoid accidents, secure them to the floor with double-faced tape, Velcro strips, or nonslip backing. If your rug is a valuable antique or seems fragile in any way, don't put it in a spot that gets a lot of traffic.

The different types of area rugs (some may be room size) include traditional pile rugs; braided, hooked, and rag rugs; needlework rugs; and flat weaves and dhurries. Pile rugs, made by knotting tufts of wool and sometimes other fibers, such as silk, encompass several different types. Oriental or Persian carpets are probably the best known. The value of these rugs, which are most often made in the Middle East and Asia, is determined by their age and the number of knots per square inch. Other types of pile rugs include cut-pile French Savonnerie rugs, Greek flokatis (which are extremely shaggy), and Scandinavian rya rugs. Machine-made pile rugs are available in all of the styles mentioned above.

Braided, hooked, and rag rugs are traditionally made by hand from scraps of fabric or yarn, although they are available in machine-made versions as well. Braided rugs are made from lengths of fabric that are gathered to make a flat round or oval coil, which is then sewn together to make the rug. Hooked rugs are made from scraps or tufts worked through a canvas backing. The pile may be looped or cut. Rag rugs are woven of multicolored strips of fabric, usually cotton, and are often striped. They have a ridged surface and are reversible.

Needlework rugs, which have a needlepoint or embroidered design, are collector's items if made in England or France in the eighteenth and nineteenth centuries. Modern versions, which are less expensive, are made in Portugal and Romania. Flat-weave rugs, such as kilims, are made of cotton or wool and have no pile. They are generally much less expensive than other types of rugs, although antique versions are expensive. Kilims are distinguished by geometric designs and rich colors. Dhurries, another type of flat-weave rug, are made in India. They are often reversible and come in a wide range of colors and patterns.

EXERCISES

Floors, although lowly and trodden on, are as important a part of your home as any other. Don't sweep them under the carpet (pun intended). Instead, treat them with care and attention. Look for areas that need fixing. Make sure your baseboards are in good shape and that floorboards are not cracked or missing. Whether you select wall-to-wall wool broadloom, slate or granite tiles, or heavy-duty vinyl, always buy the best materials you can afford, as they will last longer. The exercises that follow will help you get started and keep you on track.

1. Take yourself on a tour through your home and look at your floors. Check carefully for wear, fading, scars, holes, and other signs of deterioration. In some cases the existing floor may need only cleaning or refinishing, particularly in the case of wooden floors. Make a list of the changes, large or small, you want to make.

2. Use this chart to keep track of what flooring materials will be used in each room:

Room Type	Brand	Color	Amount	Cost

19

DECORATIVE ACCESSORIES

While furniture, paint, wallpaper, carpeting, and lighting all do their part to make a room comfortable and attractive, it's the decorative accessories—pictures, collectibles, accent pieces—that really give it personality. Much can be done to create an inviting atmosphere with an artful grouping of candles of varying sizes and shapes in beautiful holders. And don't underestimate the effect of a collection of mirrors on the wall or plants arranged around a window. Just remember to choose your decorative pieces according to your own tastes, not according to fashion. Nothing dates more quickly or seems more impersonal than a room filled with all the "latest" things.

DISPLAYING COLLECTIONS

There are two schools of thought in regard to decorating with collectibles. One school opts for simplicity: less is more. The fewer items you have on display, the more you will see them. The other school, of course, leans to the opposite point of view: everything out in sight, massed together to create texture and variety. Of course, if you take the first route, you must make certain that your pieces are really worth the attention; otherwise they will seem cheap and uninteresting.

CHECKLIST

1. Are fragile items placed out of harm's way?
2. If you have a collection of some kind, is it properly lit?
3. Is there room for both your decorative pieces and ordinary items, such as magazines, books, and coffee cups?
4. Do pictures hang straight and at their best level? Are other wall-mounted items in the optimum spot?
5. Do frames and mats harmonize with other room furnishings or details?

Conversely, if you go for number and variety, you will need to make sure that the objects are displayed in an interesting, thoughtful way or the effect will just be cluttered.

If you are dealing with a large collection of items, there are at least three basic ways of organizing it: by color, by size, or by type. The first two often work quite dramatically, but if the items you collect tend to be diverse, you may want to take the third option, grouping like with like.

Depending on the size and nature of your collectibles, you have a few choices of how to display them. If the objects are extremely fragile, don't place them on low tables or shelves where they might be brushed against and knocked over. Instead put them in vitrines, in glass-front cabinets, or on shelves that are high enough to keep them out of harm's way. If the items in your collection would benefit from being seen from various angles, you might want to display them on glass shelves. Bookshelves are another good place to display small items, but not fragile ones, especially if books are removed and replaced frequently.

A fireplace provides many decorating opportunities. The mantel and wall above it are a traditional place to display decorative objects and framed works of art. Functional items such as fireplace tools and andirons can be considered decorative accessories too. Choose them according to the style and color scheme of the living room.

PICTURES AND PICTURE FRAMES

You can frame anything that's fairly flat, from prints and drawings to sheet music covers, postcards, and autographed menus. You can get custom-made frames at a frame shop, but they can be expensive, depending on the size of the item to be framed. A quicker and simpler alternative is to clamp the piece between a sheet of glass or Plexiglas and a thin piece of board or even heavy cardboard. An art supply store will carry all of the items you need to do this, and some may even cut glass to order. An alternative recommended by Martha Stewart is to use two pieces of glass or clear plastic and seal the edges with metallic tape, creating a see-through frame. Homemade frames such as these can be displayed in easels on a table or hung from a decorative hanger attached to the top edge of the frame.

Antique textiles also look great hung on the wall. Heavy items, such as quilts or rugs, can be hung from curtain rods fixed to the wall. Smaller items, such as pieces of old lace, may be framed.

If you have a collection of prints, photographs, drawings, or paintings, you will want to hang them in a way that shows them off to their best advantage. If the collection has a central theme and the items are all approximately the same size, then it's easy to pick appropriate frames and mats and hang them in a group. If the items in the collection vary, then it is even more important to choose a harmonious mat shade (perhaps one that goes with the room rather than different ones chosen to suit each item perfectly) and frame style in order to give unity to the collection.

When hanging framed items, whatever their pictorial content or style, there are certain rules to follow. Don't hang things so close together that they seem crowded or so far apart that they look scattered on a vast expanse of wall. Don't hang them so high up they can't seen or so low that people seated on a sofa or chair might knock their heads against the bottom of the frame. Vertical arrangements of frames suggest height, while horizontal arrangements make a room or wall seem wider. A diverse group of sizes and shapes looks best contained within a circular, square, or triangular frame configuration.

LIGHTING

Lighting your collection or decorative accents gives them importance. If they can't be properly seen, they won't look good. If your objects are displayed on a glass shelf, you might try lighting them from below; this works especially well for glass objects. If your shelving is opaque you will have to light from above; you can use a downlight or spot or attach picture lights or strip lighting to the underside of the shelves (see Chapter 16, "Lighting," for more information).

EXERCISES

1. In order to create a suitable wall arrangement, you can experiment by laying the framed works down on the floor or a tabletop and arranging them to your satisfaction. That way you won't have to make any irrevocable holes in the wall before you know exactly what you're doing. Once you've arranged them on the floor, measure the distances between the items and make a sketch to scale. Then you can translate the arrangement exactly onto the wall.

2. Take out all of your decorative items and arrange them on a large, flat surface, such as a large table or the floor. Look them over to see what goes with what. It's a good idea to pick out smaller groups and have another table or counter nearby to use for creating these smaller groupings. In this way you'll get fresh ideas for tabletop groupings as well as some notions for new objects you may want to acquire.

APPENDIX A
Working with a Design Professional

✦ ✦ ✦ ✦ ✦ ✦ ✦ ✦ ✦ ✦ ✦ ✦ ✦ ✦ ✦ ✦

When planning the decoration or redecoration of your home, you may feel you need more help than your family, your best friend, or decorating books can give you. You may want to hire a professional designer or decorator to help out, whether it's for relatively simple tasks, such as finding the perfect fabric for a slipcover, or the purchase of furniture, carpeting, and window treatments for an entire house. If you feel you don't have the time or the expertise to complete a decorating project on your own, a professional can become your partner and facilitator in the design and decorating process and help you achieve your goals.

If the idea that a designer or decorator's services are too expensive is stopping you, think again. If it's a choice between a comfortable, attractive room and your current mess, it's worth checking out the various levels of design assistance available. You don't have to hire a nationally known architect or designer to redo your living room. In every area there are a number of architects, designers, and decorators who specialize in small-scale residential projects. Some even specialize in particular rooms, such as certified kitchen and bath designers.

The best way to hire a designer or decorator is to ask around. Ask your friends, relatives, and co-workers if they have worked with a designer or decorator whose services they would recommend. In addition, look in the yellow pages under any of these headings: architects, designers, interior design, home design, home decorating, furniture, or fabrics, depending on the scale of your project. As a guarantee of knowledge and reliability, look for designers who are associated with a professional organization, such as the American Society of Interior Designers (ASID) or the International Society of Interior Designers (ISID).

Put together a list of likely prospects and then interview them. Assemble as much specific information as you can on the size and scope of your project (it will help if you have completed a personal inventory and drawn a floor plan—see Chapter 1) before approaching a designer or decorator. It will also help if you can supply them with photographs of the existing room or rooms. Go to their offices and meet with them. If you find one who seems sympathetic and a person you might want to work with, have him or her come to your home for a second interview. Speak to designers and decorators directly, not to salespeople. Ask about their experience and education. Look through their portfolios of past projects and discuss those you find appealing. Ask them to explain anything you don't understand. Ask specific questions about projects to find out more about how well they communicate. If they can't tell you clearly how a project came to look as it did, they will probably have similar difficulties communicating with you on your project. Ask for references, and be sure to call more than one reference to get as much information as you need.

Once you have interviewed a number of different prospects, ask yourself these questions:

1. Does the designer or decorator listen well when you express your wants and needs?
2. Does he or she express enthusiasm for the project?
3. Is the designer qualified to handle the project?
4. Do you feel you can work well with this person?

It's important that you feel you have some kind of rapport and are comfortable with your designer or decorator. Depending on the nature and size of the project, you will be working together for weeks or months at a time. Another problem, of course, is the budget, which must accommodate your designer's fee. There are a number of different ways designers and decorators may charge for their services. Some charge a fixed fee, some bill on a cost-plus basis (that is, the cost of an item, such as fabric or furniture, plus a 15 to 20 percent fee), on an hourly basis, or on a percentage basis (the designer's fee is a percentage of the final cost of the project).

The type of billing depends on the type of project. A large project might be billed in several different ways. However, most small residential projects not involving remodeling are billed on a cost-plus, hourly, or fixed-fee basis. If the designer or decorator is finding items such as furniture, fabric, or decorative accessories for you, or having them made, these charges may well be figured on a cost-plus basis. The drawing of plans and the making of color boards is most often billed by the hour. Consultations, no matter how long they take, may be done for a flat fee. Each designer or decorator has his or her own fee structure, so it's best to discuss it up front, before a commitment is made.

In addition you will need to discuss a budget. Don't be shy. Almost no one has enough money to achieve a dream home. A good designer will encourage you to discuss your budget thoroughly, help you figure out your priorities, and help you make smart choices so you can get what you want and need and still stay within your means.

APPENDIX B

Sample Budget for a Living Room

✦ ✦ ✦ ✦ ✦ ✦ ✦ ✦ ✦ ✦ ✦ ✦ ✦ ✦ ✦ ✦

Under "Estimated Cost" list what you would like to be able to spend, given the cost of items you have seen in the stores and in catalogs, and under "Budgeted Cost" list the amounts you can realistically spend.

Budget Item	*Estimated Cost*	*Budgeted Cost*
FURNITURE		
Lamp table	$300	$250
Coffee table	$899	$500
Ottoman	$750	$400
FABRIC		
Slipcovers	12 yards @ $25/yard = $300	$250
Window treatments (2)	16 yards @ $38/yard = $608	$500
LIGHTING		
New fixtures (ceiling mounted)	3 @ $72 each = $216	$150
Decorative Fixtures	2 @ $99 each = $198; 2 @ $280 each = $560 Total: $758	$700

(continued)

FLOORING		
Area rug (8 feet by 10 feet)	$1,200	$600
WALLS		
Paint (1 gallon covers approximately 600 to 650 square feet)	1 gallon @ $32 (Walls); 1 quart @ $16 (Trim) Total: $48	$100
LABOR		
Slipcovers	$500	$500
Window treatments	$800	$750
Painting	$400 (16 hours @ $25/hour)	$500
TOTAL	$6,779	$5,200

APPENDIX C
Sample Cost Breakdown

✦ ✦ ✦ ✦ ✦ ✦ ✦ ✦ ✦ ✦ ✦ ✦ ✦ ✦ ✦ ✦

Interior designers and decorators may charge for their services in a number of ways. If your designer is working for a flat fee, you should compose a letter of agreement stating the services the designer will perform for that fee. If the designer charges by the hour or on a percentage or cost-plus basis, he or she should submit a "cost breakdown," which states the services to be performed and an estimate of how much they will cost. A designer's proposed budget may include some or all of the following items:

Item	*Cost*
Schematic design	______________
Design development	______________
Preparation of documents	______________
Interior paint	______________

Item	*Cost*
Wallpaper	______
Flooring (hardwood)	______
Flooring (carpet)	______
Flooring (vinyl)	______
Flooring (tile)	______
Plastic laminate	______
Hardware	______
Light fixtures	______
Labor	______
Extras	______
Subtotal	______
Overhead	______
Total before taxes	______
Designer's fee (percentage)	______
Sales tax	______
TOTAL	______

APPENDIX D
Resources

✦ ✦ ✦ ✦ ✦ ✦ ✦ ✦ ✦ ✦ ✦ ✦ ✦ ✦ ✦ ✦

A number of mail-order outlets sell factory-fresh, brand-name furniture for up to 50 percent off the suggested retail price. Following are the names and phone numbers of a few well-regarded discount furniture retailers. Call or write them for more information, such as brochures or catalogs.

Annex Furniture Galleries
P.O. Box 958
High Point, NC 27261
(800) 334-7391

Cherry Hill Furniture
P.O. Box 7405
High Point, NC 27264
(800) 328-0933

Edgar B
P.O. Box 849
Clemmons, NC 27012
(800) 255-6589

Homeway Furniture Co.
121 W. Lebanon St.
Mount Airy, NC 27030
(800) 334-9094

North Carolina Furniture Showrooms
1805 NW 38th Ave.
Lauderhill, FL 33311
(800) 227-6060
(They also have retail showrooms in many cities.)

Mail-order sources for furniture, tabletop, linens, decorative accessories, rugs, and ready-made window treatments:

Chambers: (800) 334-9790 for catalog or to order. Bed and bath (bed linens, towels, furniture, decorative accessories).

Crate & Barrel: (800) 323-5461 for free catalog, store locations, or to place an order. Furniture, tabletop, rugs, decorative accessories.

Domestications: (800) 746-2555 for catalog. Bed linens, tabletop, decorative accessories, rugs, and window treatments.

Eddie Bauer Home Collection: (800) 426-8020 for free catalog and store locations. Furniture, bedding, decorative accessories.

Ethan Allen: (203) 743-8000 for store locations. Furniture and decorative accessories.

Frontgate: (800) 626-6488 for catalog. Upscale home accessories.

Gardener's Eden: (800) 822-9600 for catalog or to order. Tabletop, decorative accessories, indoor/outdoor furniture, gardening equipment.

Leathercraft: (800) 951-3507 for catalog ($10) and video. Upholstered leather seating. Mailing address: P.O. Box 639, Conover, NC 28613.

Pier One Imports: (800) 447-4371 for mailing list and store locations. Furniture, tabletop, linens, decorative accessories.

Pottery Barn: (800) 922-5507 for catalog and store locations. Upholstered furniture, case goods, ready-made window treatments, tabletop, linens, rugs, decorative accessories.

Room & Board: (800) 486-6554 for store information. Furniture, decorative accessories.

Smith & Hawken: (800) 776-3336 for catalog. Indoor/outdoor furniture, decorative accessories, all with gardening theme.

Storehouse: (800) 869-2468 for catalog and store locations. Furniture, decorative accessories.

Williams-Sonoma: (800) 541-1262 for catalog. Tabletop, cook's tools, kitchen accessories.

Workbench: (800) 767-1710 for catalog and store locations. Upholstered furniture, case goods, rugs, decorative accessories.

ANNOTATED BIBLIOGRAPHY

✦ ✦ ✦ ✦ ✦ ✦ ✦ ✦ ✦ ✦ ✦ ✦ ✦ ✦ ✦ ✦

GENERAL

Battersby, Martin. *The Decorative Thirties*. Revised and edited by Philippe Garner. New York: Whitney Library of Design, 1988.

———. *The Decorative Twenties*. Revised and edited by Philippe Garner. New York: Whitney Library of Design, 1988.

Both of these books are well-illustrated guides to furniture, color schemes, wallpaper, textiles, and decorative objects of the twenties or thirties.

Calloway, Stephen, and Stephen Jones. *Style Traditions: Recreating Period Interiors*. New York: Rizzoli, 1990.

Written by two English decorative arts historians, this guide to creating a period interior includes tips on modern substitutes for authenticity.

Conran, Terence. *The New House Book.* New York: Crown Publishing Group, 1985.

This update of a classic late-1960s decorating guide by British designer and entrepreneur Terence Conran serves as a useful reference, especially for its many photographs.

Garey, Carol Cooper. *House Beautiful Decorating Style.* New York: William Morris, 1992.

Useful most for its many beautiful photos, which provide plenty of inspiration. There is also a directory of designers and architects. Other books in the House Beautiful *series include* Kitchens *and* Color.

Gilliatt, Mary. *Complete Book of Home Design.* Revised edition. Boston: Little, Brown, 1989.

———. *The Decorating Book.* New York: Pantheon Books, 1982.

———. *New Guide to Decorating.* Revised edition. Boston: Little, Brown, 1988.

These are just a few of the many books on home design by British interior decorator Mary Gilliatt. Other titles include Dream Houses, English Country Style, Setting Up Home, *and* The Mary Gilliatt Book of Color. *All are useful and detailed.*

———. *Decorating with Mary Gilliatt.* Boston: Little, Brown, 1992.

Contains many of the ideas presented in her other books, but in condensed form. It has many useful checklists and accompanied the PBS television series of the same name.

Hogg, Min, Wendy Harrop, and *The World of Interiors. Interiors.* New York: Clarkson N. Potter, 1988.

Illustrations of interiors from the sleek, sophisticated publication the World of Interiors, *based in London. The photos were selected by the magazine's editor and former editor, who provide commentary.*

Iovine, Julie. *Chic Simple Home.* New York: Alfred A. Knopf, 1993.

Billed as "a decorating guide for the 1990s," this book is useful for its up-to-date suggestions and good source list.

Kent, Kathryn. *The Good Housekeeping Guide to Traditional American Decorating.* New York: Hearst Books, 1982.

Although written more than a decade ago, this is still a good, thorough guide to traditional American interiors, containing lots of practical advice.

Klein, Dan, Nancy A. McClelland, and Malcolm Haslam. *In the Deco Style.* New York: Rizzoli, 1987.

Profusely illustrated guide on adapting the deco look to present-day interiors.

McCloud, Kevin. *Decorative Style.* New York: Simon and Schuster, 1990.

A comprehensive source book on creating historical styles, with complete instructions on paint treatments, color schemes, techniques, and materials, written by a set designer and art historian who combines practical knowledge of traditional paints, varnishes, and solvents with a thorough understanding of the history of design.

Mayer, Barbara. *In the Arts and Crafts Style.* San Francisco: Chronicle Books, 1992.

A beautifully illustrated source book for re-creating the popular Arts and Crafts style.

Ruggiero, Joseph. *Found Objects: A Style and Source Book.* New York: Clarkson N. Potter, 1981.

Plenty of photographs of interiors by well-known designers. The book supplies ideas on how to decorate with collections, found objects, and industrial leftovers.

Slesin, Suzanne. *The New York Times Home Book of Modern Design: Styles, Problems, and Solutions.* New York: Random House, 1982.

Although out of print, this book can be found in libraries and is a useful source of information on creating a modern interior.

———. *Caribbean Style.* New York: Crown Publishing Group, 1985.

———. *English Style.* New York: Crown Publishing Group, 1984.

———. *French Style.* New York: Crown Publishing Group, 1982.

———. *Greek Style.* New York: Crown Publishing Group, 1988.

———. *Indian Style.* New York: Crown Publishing Group, 1990.

———. *Japanese Style.* New York: Crown Publishing Group, 1988.

———. *Spanish Style.* New York: Crown Publishing Group, 1990.

This series of style books by decorating writer Slesin, who also writes for the New York Times, *provides plenty of inspiration.*

Stoddard, Alexandra. *Creating a Beautiful Home.* New York: William Morrow, 1992.
The latest book by this prolific author. Although written in a flowery style, it does give good, specific advice. Best for those interested in creating a traditional, rather formal interior. Has watercolor drawings instead of photos.

Wissinger, Joanna. *Lost and Found: Decorating with Unexpected Objects.* New York: Macmillan, 1991.
A lively, profusely illustrated guide to decorating with collections, folk art, architectural salvage, and found objects. The case studies in the second half are particularly useful.

———. *Victorian Details: Enhancing Antique and Contemporary Homes with Period Accents.* New York: Dutton, 1990.
A useful and well-illustrated guide to re-creating Victorian-style interiors.

KIDS' ROOMS

Aria, Barbara. *Nursery Design: Creating a Perfect Environment for Your Child.* New York: Bantam Books, 1990.
A thoughtful guide to decorating babies' rooms.

Fisher, Rosie. *Decorative Painting for Children's Rooms.* Cincinnati: North Light Books, 1990.
Information on creating painted decorations for children's rooms, including murals.

Torrice, Antonio, and Ro Logrippo. *In My Room: Designing for and with Children.* New York: Fawcett Columbine, 1989.
Cowritten by a designer who is also an early childhood specialist and by a design writer, this book comes highly recommended by anyone who has ever used it.

ORGANIZATION AND STORAGE

Coen, Patricia, and Brian Milford. *Closets: Designing and Organizing the Personalized Closet.* New York: Grove Weidenfeld, 1988.

With lots of photographs and illustrations, this is a very useful book that explains step by step how to organize your closets to suit your needs.

Schoen, Elin. *The Closet Book.* New York: Harmony Books, 1982.

This well-illustrated book offers lots of good ideas on organizing your closet.

KITCHENS AND BATHS

Conran, Terence. *The Bed and Bath Book.* New York: Crown Publishing Group, 1978.

———. *The Kitchen Book.* New York: Crown Publishing Group, 1977.

Although in need of an update, these books provide useful information and numerous inspiring photographs.

Goldbeck, David. *The Smart Kitchen.* Woodstock, N.Y.: Ceres Press, 1989.

Lots of useful information on designing and creating an environmentally correct kitchen, including information on creating workable recycling areas and the impact of various materials on the environment.

Niles, Bo, and Juta Ristsoo. *Planning the Perfect Kitchen.* New York: Simon and Schuster, 1988.

Very detailed information on the technical aspects of kitchen design. Includes a useful set of peel-and-stick templates.

DO-IT-YOURSELF

Buckingham, Sandra. *Stencilling: A Harrowsmith Guide.* Ontario, Canada: Camden House, 1989.

A thorough, thoughtful book on stenciling of all types and styles for the home.

Conran, Terence. *Terence Conran's Do-It-Yourself with Style: Original Designs for Living Rooms and Work Spaces.* New York: Fireside/Simon and Schuster, 1989.

———. *Terence Conran's Do-It-Yourself with Style: Original Designs for Bathrooms and Bedrooms.* New York: Fireside/Simon and Schuster, 1989.

———. *Terence Conran's Do-It-Yourself with Style: Original Designs for Kitchens and Dining Rooms.* New York: Fireside/Simon and Schuster, 1989.

This series of three guides offers useful tips on creating built-in storage and display areas throughout the house, with instructions on materials and techniques to re-create or adapt the designs to your own home.

Haege, Glenn. *Take the Pain Out of Painting.* New York: Master Handyman, 1993.

Very task oriented, but really gives you the basics on how to be your own painting contractor.

Innes, Jocasta. *Decorating with Paint.* New York: Random House, 1989.

More detailed than her popular Paint Magic.

———. *Paint Magic.* New York: Pantheon Books, 1981.

Inspiring guide to creating your own decorative painted finishes.

Paine, Melanie. *Fabric Magic.* New York: Pantheon Books, 1987.

A terrific guide to conceiving and making your own soft furnishings, from curtains and drapes to pillows and comforter covers, as well as simple slipcovers and room screens.

REFERENCE

Fairbanks, Jonathan L., and Elizabeth Bidwell Bates. *American Furniture: 1620 to the Present.* New York: Richard Marek, 1981.

A guide to American style from colonial times to the present.

Fleming, John, and Hugh Honour. *The Penguin Dictionary of Decorative Arts.* Revised edition. New York: Viking Penguin, 1989.

A comprehensive guide to decorative objects, including rugs, furniture, and ceramics.

Pile, John. *Dictionary of 20th-Century Design.* New York: Facts On File, 1990.

A guide to objects and designers of the twentieth century.

White, Antony, and Bruce Robertson. *Architecture and Ornament: A Visual Guide.* New York: Design Press, 1990.

———. *Furniture and Furnishings: A Visual Guide.* New York: Design Press, 1990.

Using outline drawings, these guides provide information on ornament (moldings, door frames, and other details) and furnishings.

PUBLICATIONS

Decorating magazines are a good source of inspiration. Those listed below are easy to find on the newsstand or in the library.

Architectural Digest

Very elegant, high-end design.

Classic Home

Traditional design; published only a few times a year.

Colonial Homes

Bimonthly; focuses on traditional design and crafts.

Decorating Remodeling
Has a practical orientation.

Elle Decor
Elegant design with a European slant. Published six times a year.

Home
Focuses on contemporary, affordable design.

House Beautiful
Features expensive homes by prominent decorators. Frequently includes information on environmentally correct design.

Martha Stewart Living
Lots of how-tos and tips on many topics, including cooking and entertaining as well as decorating.

Metropolis
Covers design issues of all types.

Traditional Home
As the name suggests, concentrates on traditional design.

Victoria
Decorating is merely one of the many "lifestyle" topics covered in this popular publication.

PROFESSIONAL JOURNALS

You will have to look for these in a specialty bookstore or in the library.

Architectural Record
Has special issues on interiors and residences.

Interior Design
The foremost journal for professional interior designers.

Interiors
Focuses on business design, with occasional residences.

Progressive Architecture
Has a special issue on interiors once a year, usually in September.

PHOTO CREDITS

✦ ✦

Page 2, copyright © John Hall; *page 34,* courtesy Village Wallpaper; *page 48,* courtesy Gramercy; *page 68,* copyright © John Hall; *page 80,* copyright © John Hall; *page 88,* courtesy Smallbone/Siematic; *page 97*, courtesy Smallbone/ Siematic; *page 106*, copyright © Armstrong; *page 114*, courtesy IKEA; *page 124,* courtesy IKEA; *page 134,* copyright © John Hall; *page 146,* courtesy Village Wallpaper; *page 156,* courtesy IKEA; *page 163,* courtesy IKEA; *page 168,* courtesy Whirlpool Corporation; *page 178*, courtesy IKEA; *page 190,* copyright © John Hall; *page 212,* copyright © John Hall; *page 224,* courtesy Village Wallpaper; *page 234,* courtesy IKEA; *page 244,* courtesy Village Wallpaper.